ROCK LYRICS QUIZ BOOK

"featuring pop/rock stars from the 1970s"

250 ROCK LYRICS QUESTIONS/ 250 ROCK TITLES QUESTIONS

an encyclopedia of rock & roll's most memorable lyrics in question/answer format

by: Presley Love

Published by Hi-Lite Publishing Co.

Copyright © 2015, 2018 by:
Raymond Karelitz
Hi-Lite Publishing Company
Rock-&-Roll Test Prep Hawaii
P.O. Box 6071
Kaneohe, Hawaii 96744

```
* * * * * * * * * * * * * * * * * * * * * * * * * *
*    If you liked this book,    *
*  please share your comments   *
*         on AMAZON.com         *
*        for others to see      *
* * * * * * * * * * * * * * * * * * * * * * * * * *
```

email comments/corrections: rocknrolltriviaquizbook.com
(808) 261-6666

All rights reserved. No part of this book may be reproduced in any form or by any means—except brief excerpts for promotional purposes—without permission in writing from the publisher.

We encourage all readers to listen to your oldies records while perusing this book. However, public performance of most songs is under copyright restriction by ASCAP/BMI; extensive replication of lyrics is restricted under copyright of the writer and/or publisher.

4th EDITION -- Updated Printing: 2019

Love, Presley

ROCK LYRICS & TITLES QUIZ BOOK (1970-1979)
(128 pages)

1. Rock-&-Roll Quiz Book   I. Love, Presley   II. Title: Rock and Roll

2. Music

COVER DESIGN: *Doug Behrens*

ISBN: 978-1516842797

Printed In The United States of America

A Magical Musical Tour Through the Past

Once you open this book, you will be transported back to the time of magical musical memories, a mosaic of music at your fingertips!

Browse through the streets where the '70s still rule. Test your rock-trivia expertise — invite your friends to see who's the ROCK LYRIC KING!

Rock & Roll is here to stay, and now every memory-making word can be recalled whenever you feel like escaping to the past, groovin' where no person has gone before! Put on your oldies records, let their words of wisdom come alive for you, then sit back in ecstasy and let the good vibrations take you on a magic swirling ship headed on a collision course with the classics!

****

To be best prepared for this book, listen to lots of rock & roll — heavily energized with the Doobie Brothers, Eagles and America — and don't forget to get out your high-top Elton John boogie shoes and bell-bottoms . . . For added flavor, light a stick of incense and turn on your strobe light!

---

text collection by: **Presley Love**
format/production by: Raymond Karelitz

The Legacy of Presley Love

In 1992, music-aficionado Presley Love compiled a vast treasure of rock & roll lyric-memoribilia, including songs from the earliest days of rock & roll up through the late '80s. This musical quiz-format collection lay dormant except for the release of a single volume which contained 400 questions. The original book — printed in 1992 — became, over the years, an Amazon.com favorite, with very positive response from those who loved the book for its "party-flavor" appeal.

In 2014, the entire vault of Presley Love's music-lyric memoribilia was located in a storage locker — containing his collection of lyric-questions and trivia questions in quiz format! After four years of diligent compiling and organizing, the entire Presley Love collection of rock lyrics, rock titles and rock group trivia is now available in quiz-format!

We are proud to unveil *ROCK LYRICS & TITLES TRIVIA QUIZ BOOK* (1970-1979), a special volume of this rare and collectible series. We sincerely hope you enjoy these fabulous rock-favorites in quiz-format from Presley Love's truly incredible treasure trove of rock & roll memories 1955-1989 collection!

ROCK LYRICS QUESTIONS

If you're brave enough to test your skills,
here's a simple SCORING CHART:

(questions are worth 1 point each — "Harder Questions" are worth 2 points each . . . If you are able to correctly answer the question without referring to the three choices, you receive twice the point value!)

If you score . . .

    25+ Points: You probably STILL think it's 1975!
(Check your wardrobe!)

    20-24: You probably paid more attention to
rock & roll than books & school!
(Check your report card!)

    15-19: There's a lot of rock & roll memories
in your blood!
*(But maybe it's time to buy
a few more rock & roll CDs
& put on your boogie shoes!)*

    10-14: Don't you wish you'd listened more closely
to rock & roll?!
(It's never too late to be hip!)

    0-9: Where were YOU when rock began to rule?!
*(Time to get experienced —
run to your music store now!!!)*

(note: all answers are derived from lyrics within the song)

1. What does Bobby Sherman tell his *Little Woman* that she's got to do ?
   a. come into his world and leave her world behind ✓
   b. quit telling lies and stop going out with other guys
   c. grow up

****

2. Because you've got your *Backfield in Motion*, what are Mel & Tim going to have to do ?
   a. kick you in the rear
   b. penalize you ✓
   c. shut off your engine

****

3. In *Whole Lotta Love*, what does Led Zeppelin say they're going to do ?
   a. make love to you all night long
   b. send you back to schoolin' ✓
   c. come a-callin'

****

4. In *Sweet Caroline*, what happens to Neil Diamond's hurt when he's holding you ?
   a. it turns to happiness
   b. it shimmies down his backbone
   c. it runs off his shoulders ✓

****

5. According to Bread, *It Don't Matter to Me* if you _____.
   a. need some time to be free ✓
   b. really love him
   c. don't know how to dance

6. In *Instant Karma (We All Shine On)*, what does John Lennon say that you are ?
   - a. a superstar ✓
   - b. a dreamer ✓
   - c. a ray of hope on a cloudy day

****

7. Because *Eli's Coming*, what do Three Dog Night say you've got to hide ?
   - a. the truth ✓
   - b. your pocketbook ✗
   - ✓ c. your heart

****

8. According to Edwin Starr, what is *War* good for ?
   - a. preserving peace
   - b. reducing the population ✓
   - c. absolutely nothing ✓

****

9. What does Chicago want you to *Color My World* with ?
   - a. with colors of blue and green ✓
   - ✓ b. with hope of loving you   ✗
   - c. with thoughts and dreams that one day may come true

****

10. In *Close to You*, what do the Carpenters say the angels sprinkled in your hair to create a dream come true ?
    - a. snowflakes ✓
    - b. magic glitter   ✗
    - ✓ c. moondust

11. In *I Want You Back*, what do the Jackson Five ask you for?
    a. one more chance ✓
    b. one more night
    c. your pledge of love

    ✓

*****

12. What would Bread give *Everything I Own* for?
    a. another kiss
    b. a chance to win your love
    c. just to have you back again ✓

    ✓

*****

13. In *Build Me Up, Buttercup,* what time do you tell the Foundations that you'll be over — even though you're always late?
    ✓ a. 10:00
    b. 8:00
    c. noon ✓

    ✗

*****

14. According to Undisputed Truth, what is it that *Smiling Faces Sometimes* don't tell?
    a. who really loves you
    b. the truth ✓
    c. the hurt that's deep inside

    ✓

*****

15. In *Get Ready*, what does Rare Earth reply when asked who it is that makes their dreams real?
    ✓ a. you do
    b. any girl who says hello
    c. the guardian angel up above ✓

    ✗

-3-

16. In *My Baby Loves Lovin'*, White Plains says their girlfriend has got what it takes and she knows how to _____.
   a. show it off
   b. dance
   c. use it ✓

17. Because Johnny Nash says *I Can See Clearly Now*, what kind of day does he see coming ?
   a. a day filled with clouds and rain
   b. a day when he can see for miles
   c. a bright, sunshiny day ✓

18. In *All Right Now*, what did Free think she might be in need of ?
   a. a friend ✓
   b. a kiss ✓
   c. a shoulder to lean on

19. In *Band of Gold*, where does Freda Payne wait, hoping for her husband to return ?
   a. in the bathroom
   b. in the hotel lobby
   c. in her room ✓

20. In *More Today Than Yesterday*, what happens every time Spiral Staircase kisses your lips ?
   a. they begin to feel weak inside ✓
   b. their mind starts to wander ✓
   c. it tastes sweeter than the time before

HARDER QUESTIONS: Worth 2 points each — 4 points if you can answer the question without the three choices !

****

1. According to Bread in *Make It With You,* who are dreams for ?
    - a. they're for the lonely ones
    - b. they're for those who sleep ✓
    - c. they're for frustrated losers

****

2. In *Do You Know What I Mean*, who was stepping out with Lee Michaels' girlfriend ?
    - a. Tommy
    - b. Sally
    - c. Bobby ✓

****

3. How has Joe Cocker found his *Delta Lady* many times in the garden ?
    - ✓ a. wet and naked
    - b. alone and afraid ✓
    - c. soft and lovely

****

4. In *What's Going On*, what does Marvin Gaye say we need here today ?
    - ✓ a. understanding
    - b. a way to find peace ✓
    - c. political honesty

****

5. In the song, what was the actual first name of Badfinger's girl whom they referred to as *Baby Blue* ?
    - ✓ a. Dixie
    - b. Susie ✓
    - c. Bonnie

ANSWERS

****

1. a. come into his world and leave her world behind
2. b. penalize you
3. b. send you back to schoolin'
4. c. it runs off his shoulders
5. a. need some time to be free
6. a. a superstar
7. c. your heart
8. c. absolutely nothing
9. b. with hope of loving you
10. c. moondust
11. a. one more chance
12. c. just to have you back again
13. a. 10:00
14. b. the truth
15. a. you do
16. c. use it
17. c. a bright, sunshiny day
18. b. a kiss
19. c. in her room
20. b. their mind starts to wander

****

HARDER QUESTIONS--Answers

1. b. they're for those who sleep
2. c. Bobby
3. a. wet and naked
4. a. understanding
5. a. Dixie

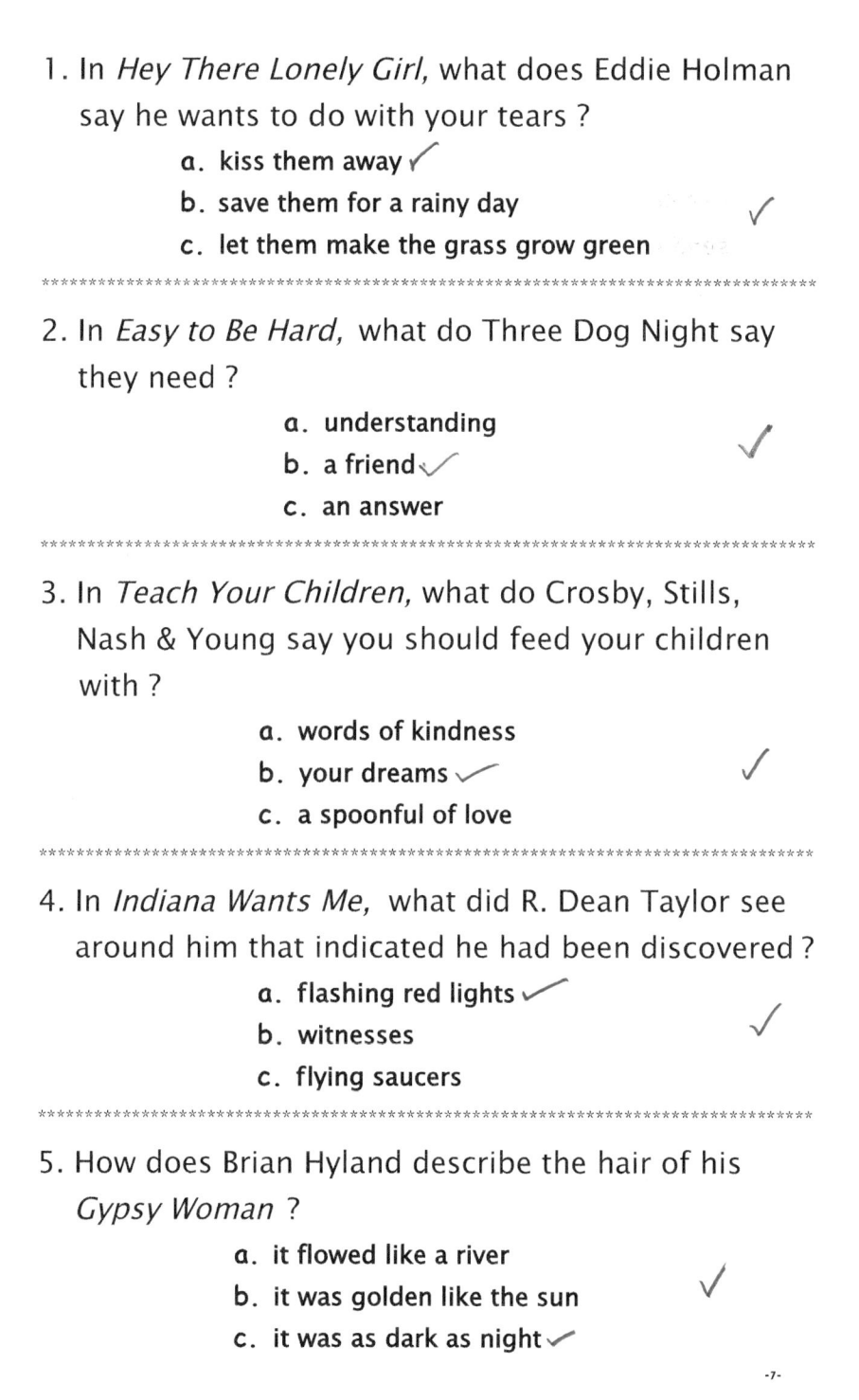

1. In *Hey There Lonely Girl*, what does Eddie Holman say he wants to do with your tears ?
    a. kiss them away ✓
    b. save them for a rainy day   ✓
    c. let them make the grass grow green

2. In *Easy to Be Hard*, what do Three Dog Night say they need ?
    a. understanding
    b. a friend ✓   ✓
    c. an answer

3. In *Teach Your Children*, what do Crosby, Stills, Nash & Young say you should feed your children with ?
    a. words of kindness
    b. your dreams ✓   ✓
    c. a spoonful of love

4. In *Indiana Wants Me*, what did R. Dean Taylor see around him that indicated he had been discovered ?
    a. flashing red lights ✓
    b. witnesses   ✓
    c. flying saucers

5. How does Brian Hyland describe the hair of his *Gypsy Woman* ?
    a. it flowed like a river
    b. it was golden like the sun   ✓
    c. it was as dark as night ✓

6. What does Van Morrison say the *Wild Night* is doing?
   - a. calling ✓
   - b. driving him wild ✓
   - c. raising the dead

   ✗

7. In *Live and Let Die,* what does Paul McCartney say you used to say?
   - a. live and let live ✓
   - b. let bygones be bygones
   - c. it's a dog-eat-dog world

   ✓

8. In *Everything Is Beautiful,* Ray Stevens says that there is none so blind as he who _____.
   - a. refuses to greet a friend
   - b. cannot love
   - c. will not see ✓

   ✓

9. According to Michael Jackson, what would most people do to *Ben*?
   - a. put him down
   - b. turn him away ✓
   - c. put him in a cage

   ✓

10. What lesson did Rick Nelson learn in *Garden Party*?
    - a. that you can't play when it rains
    - b. that not all good times happen indoors
    - c. that you can't please everyone ✓

    ✓

11. What is *Anticipation* making Carly Simon do?
	a. sweat ✓
	b. reconsider her options
	c. wait ✓

****

12. Not only is it that *You Are The Sunshine of My Life*, but what else does Stevie Wonder call you?
	a. the rose in his garden
	b. the apple of his eye ✓
	c. a beacon of hope in the dark sky

****

13. *In the Summertime*, what is Mungo Jerry's philosophy about life?
	a. life is for living ✓
	b. life's a gas
	c. you only really live in the summertime ✓

****

14. Why is that the Partridge Family says *I Woke Up in Love This Morning*?
	a. because they forgot to take a cold shower the night before
	b. because they had the sweetest dream about you
	c. because they fell asleep with you on their mind ✓

****

15. How does America describe the heat as they travel in the desert on *A Horse With No Name*?
	a. as an oppressive barrier to hope
	b. as a reminder of the stifling loneliness
	c. as hot ✓

16. According to the Eagles, what has the *Witchy Woman* got in her eyes?
    a. the moon ✓
    b. cheating
    c. the look of love

✓

****

17. In *Love Grows (Where My Rosemary Goes)*, how does Edison Lighthouse describe Rosemary's hair?
    a. it's short and cute
    b. it's wild and free ✓
    c. it's dirty and matted

✓

****

18. In *Fire and Rain*, when was James Taylor told that his woman had left him?
    a. an hour ago
    b. yesterday morning ✓
    c. last night

✓

****

19. The Dramatics say that *Whatcha See Is Whatcha Get* if you're looking for _____.
    a. real lovin' ✓
    b. jive talkin'
    c. a smooth criminal

✓

****

20. In *I've Found Someone of My Own*, what did Free Movement's mate tell them she had found?
    ✓ a. somebody to take their place
    b. a new place to stay ✓
    c. true happiness

✗

HARDER QUESTIONS: Worth 2 points each — 4 points if you can answer the question without the three choices !

****

1. In *25 or 6 to 4*, what is Chicago getting up to do ?
    - a. rearrange their life
    - b. cash in their chips
    - c. splash their face ✓   ✓

****

2. In *Baby I'm-A Want You*, Bread says that you're the only one they care enough to _____.
    - a. dream about   ✓
    - b. talk about
    - c. hurt about ✓

****

3. What does Mark Lindsay want *Arizona* to take off ?
    - a. her pretty white gown ✓
    - ✓ b. her rainbow shoes   ✗
    - c. her Panama hat

****

4. In *It's a Shame*, where are the Spinners sitting all alone ?
    - a. by the telephone ✓
    - b. in the local bar   ✓
    - c. at the restaurant

****

5. Cat Stevens' *Peace Train* lies at the edge of _____.
    - a. the tracks
    - b. darkness ✓
    - c. your mind   ✓

ANSWERS

****

1. a. kiss them away
2. b. a friend
3. b. your dreams
4. a. flashing red lights
5. c. it was as dark as night
6. a. calling
7. a. live and let live
8. c. will not see
9. b. turn him away
10. c. that you can't please everyone
11. c. wait
12. b. the apple of his eye
13. a. life is for living
14. c. because they fell asleep with you on their mind
15. c. as hot
16. a. the moon
17. b. it's wild and free
18. b. yesterday morning
19. a. real lovin'
20. a. somebody to take their place

****

HARDER QUESTIONS--Answers

1. c. splash their face
2. c. hurt about
3. b. her rainbow shoes
4. a. by the telephone
5. b. darkness

1. In *I Just Want to Celebrate,* what happened when Rare Earth put their faith in the people?
    a. the people let them down ✓
    b. they became enlightened   ✓
    c. they found a new friend

2. What does Edward Bear say regarding the *Last Song*?
    a. it's his last chance for success ✓
    ✓ b. it's the last one he'll ever write for you   ✗
    c. it wasn't as good as the next one will be

3. What does Albert Hammond say he's out of in *It Never Rains in California* that has him wanting to go home?
    a. water
    b. friends
    c. self-respect ✓   ✓

4. Because *I'm Still In Love With You,* what is Al Green doing during the day?
    a. looking for a job
    b. thinking about you ✓   ✓
    c. gazing at your picture

5. What does Jackson Browne ask in *Doctor My Eyes* whether he may have been unwise to do?
    a. listen to all the lies
    b. leave his eyes open for so long ✓   ✓
    c. fall for all of your alibis

6. Because *School's Out,* what does Alice Cooper say we won't have any more of ?
    a. friends to see or things to do
    b. education through indoctrination
    c. pencils, books, and teachers' dirty looks ✓ ✓

7. In Stephen Stills' *Love the One You're With,* where might a rose be found ?
    a. in the fisted glove ✓   ✓
    b. where you least expect it
    c. where there is love

8. According to Loggins & Messina in *Your Mama Don't Dance,* what time do the old folks want you to be home after a night of entertaining ?
    a. midnight
    b. dawn   ✓
    c. ten o'clock ✓

9. When you're not strong, Bill Withers wants you to *Lean On Me* and he'll be your _____.
    a. guiding light   ✓
    b. friend ✓
    c. partner in crime

10. Where does Todd Rundgren say *I Saw the Light* ?
    ✓ a. in your eyes   ✗
    b. in the night ✓
    c. at the end of the tunnel

11. Where are Brewer & Shipley sitting while they're
    One Toke Over the Line ?
        a. on the dock of the bay
        ✓b. in a railway station
        c. in the county jail ✓   ✗

***

12. In *Don't Let Me Be Lonely Tonight*, what does
    James Taylor say you'll never see him do ?
        a. ever desert you ✓
        b. tell you how to lead your life   ✗
        ✓ c. get down on his knees

***

13. Jim Croce's *Bad, Bad Leroy Brown* is meaner than
    _____.
        a. an angry skunk
        b. a hungry lion
        c. a junkyard dog ✓   ✓

***

14. *No Matter What* you do and who you are, what
    does Badfinger say they'll always do ?
        a. be with you ✓
        b. lend you money when you need it   ✓
        c. respect you

***

15. In *I Just Can't Help Believing*, with what does
    B. J. Thomas' heart beat ?
        a. the ticking of the clock
        b. the sound of her heartbeat   ✓
        c. the rhythm of her sigh ✓

16. With what in your voice does Neil Diamond say you can sing a *Song Sung Blue* and then start feeling good as a result?
  a. with a harmony in your voice
  b. with a cry in your voice ✓
  c. with a note of cheer

17. According to Three Dog Night, what filled the air in the room where *Mama Told Me Not to Come*?
  a. the smell of stale perfume ✓
  b. the fragrant whisper of love
  c. a haunting memory

18. Although it's *Just My Imagination*, what do the Temptations say about having a girl like her?
  a. it would send them halfway to heaven
  b. it could never happen in real life
  c. it's truly a dream come true ✓

19. In *I Feel the Earth Move*, Carole King sees your face as mellow as which month?
  a. May ✓
  b. July
  c. November

20. According to the Carpenters, *It's Going to Take Some Time* to do what?
  a. make up
  b. right the wrongs that they've done
  c. get themselves in shape ✓

HARDER QUESTIONS: Worth 2 points each — 4 points if you can answer the question without the three choices !

1. In *Beautiful,* how long does Gordon Lightfoot say you and he have been friends ?
    - a. for such a long time ✓
    - b. since last summer
    - c. since the early days

2. According to Bread, what can the *Guitar Man* do ?
    - a. give you hope and a song ✓
    - b. bring you down and get you high ✓
    - c. read your deepest thoughts

3. In *American Pie,* what did Don McLean sing in the park the day the music died ?
    - a. Buddy Holly songs
    - b. dirges ✓
    - c. the blues

4. According to Bill Withers, when is it that there *Ain't No Sunshine* ?
    - a. when it rains
    - b. when she's gone ✓
    - c. every morning when he rises

5. David Essex wants you to *Rock On* by doing what ?
    - a. jumping up and down in your blue suede shoes ✓
    - b. shaking your head while wiggling your toes
    - c. snapping your fingers and stomping your feet

ANSWERS

****

1. a. the people let them down
2. b. it's the last one he'll ever write for you
3. c. self-respect
4. b. thinking about you
5. b. leave his eyes open for so long
6. c. pencils, books, and teachers' dirty looks
7. a. in the fisted glove
8. c. ten o'clock
9. b. friend
10. a. in your eyes
11. b. in a railway station
12. c. get down on his knees
13. c. a junkyard dog
14. a. be with you
15. c. the rhythm of her sigh
16. b. with a cry in your voice
17. a. the smell of stale perfume
18. c. it's truly a dream come true
19. a. May
20. c. get themselves in shape

****

HARDER QUESTIONS--Answers

1. a. for such a long time
2. b. bring you down and get you high
3. b. dirges
4. b. when she's gone
5. a. jumping up and down in your blue suede shoes

1. Because *You've Got a Friend,* what does James Taylor say you have to do to have him come running to you ?
    a. snap your fingers
    b. call out his name ✓
    c. write him a letter

2. Olivia Newton-John wants you to *Let Me Be There* so she can take you where ?
    a. to Xanadu
    b. to that wonderland that only two can share ✓
    c. over the edge to where a new world awaits

3. What can't Harry Nilsson do *Without You* ?
    a. be happy
    b. live ✓
    c. anything

4. In *Take it Easy,* which city and state are the Eagles in when they espy a girl driving by them ?
    a. Houston, Texas
    b. Kansas City, Missouri
    c. Winslow, Arizona ✓

5. What does Marie Osmond say about the *Paper Roses* she received ?
    a. they remind her of your imitation love for her ✓
    b. they're as bogus as a two dollar bill
    c. they show how fragile love can be

6. In *Let's Stay Together*, how do you make Al Green feel ?
   - a. like a child with his toy ✓
   - ✓ b. brand new
   - c. insecure

   ✗

****

7. In *Hello, It's Me*, what does Todd Rundgren take for granted ?
   - a. that life will never reveal its mystery to him ✓
   - b. that your telephone is always busy
   - ✓ c. that you're always there but just don't care

   ✗

****

8. In *Killing Me Softly With His Song*, what does Roberta Flack say was being told with his words ?
   - a. her whole life ✓
   - b. lies and more lies
   - c. a sweet goodbye

   ✓

****

9. Although Eric Clapton says *I Shot the Sheriff*, what does he say he didn't do ?
   - a. shoot the deputy ✓
   - b. lock him up
   - c. run from the law

   ✓

****

10. In *Yesterday Once More*, what did the Carpenters do when their favorite song was played on the radio ?
    - a. they sang along ✓
    - b. they cried
    - c. they remembered the good times

    ✓

11. In *Down By the Schoolyard*, what does Paul Simon say about what his mama saw him and Julio doing?
    a. it was against the law ✓
    b. his mama used to do it, too   ✓
    c. she had no proof

12. In *Life and Breath*, what does Climax dream day after day?
    ✓ a. that you'll come back to them
    b. that there's too much pollution in the air ✓   ✗
    c. that they'll find love one day

13. In *(If Loving You Is Wrong) I Don"t Wanna Be Right*, what does Luther Ingram say he has back home?
    a. emptiness and sorrow
    b. a world without hope and dreams ✓   ✗
    ✓ c. a wife and two little children

14. In *You Don't Mess Around With Jim*, what does Jim Croce say is the real name of the country boy they call "Slim"?
    a. Leroy Brown ✓   ✗
    ✓ b. Willie McCoy
    c. Tuff McGurk

15. Every time Ringo Starr sees your face, what does the *Photograph* remind him of?
    a. what can never ever be   ✓
    b. the places where you and he used to go ✓
    c. how beautiful your smile was

16. In *Leave Me Alone (Ruby Red Dress)*, what does Helen Reddy say happens if you get too close to Ruby Red Dress ?
    a. she'll run away ✓
    b. she'll attack you   ✓
    c. you'll catch her fever

****

17. In *Danny's Song*, what astrological sun-sign is Kenny Loggin's cherished son ?
    a. Sagittarius   ✓
    b. Gemini
    c. Pisces ✓

****

18. In *Freddie's Dead*, what does Curtis Mayfield say Freddie was?
    a. a politician
    b. a police man   ✓
    c. a junkie ✓

****

19. In *Will It Go Round In Circles*, Billy Preston says he has a song but what doesn't it have ?
    a. any words ✓
    b. any message   ✗
    c. a melody

****

20. In *It's So Nice to Be With You*, Gallery says it's so nice to hear you say _____.
    a. their name ✓
    b. you're going to please them   ✗
    c. anything that's on your mind

HARDER QUESTIONS: Worth 2 points each — 4 points if you can answer the question without the three choices!

****

1. In *Lookin' Through the Eyes of Love,* what does the Partridge Family say they are, in the eyes of the world?
    a. just an ordinary family trying to make ends meet
    b. a loser justing wasting their time
    c. someone looking for love

****

2. In *Feeling Alright,* how does Joe Cocker says he's feeling?
    a. not too good
    b. he really can't say
    c. pretty fine

****

3. What is it that Neil Young has ignored which now has him searching for a *Heart of Gold*?
    a. the fact that time has passed him by
    b. a family that he had never before paid much attention to
    c. expressions he's never given

****

4. According to the Grateful Dead, *Casey Jones* is high on _____.
    a. life
    b. his own horse
    c. cocaine

****

5. In *Soolaimon,* what does Neil Diamond ask to bring home?
    a. everlasting peace
    b. a new message of hope
    c. his name

ANSWERS

****

1. b. call out his name
2. b. to that wonderland that only two can share
3. b. live
4. c. Winslow, Arizona
5. a. they remind her of your imitation love for her
6. b. brand new
7. c. that you're always there but just don't care
8. a. her whole life
9. a. shoot the deputy
10. a. they sang along
11. a. it was against the law
12. a. that you'll come back to them
13. c. a wife and two little children
14. b. Willie McCoy
15. b. the places where you and he used to go
16. a. she'll run away
17. c. Pisces
18. c. a junkie
19. c. a melody
20. b. you're going to please them

****

HARDER QUESTIONS--Answers

1. b. a loser justing wasting their time
2. a. not too good
3. c. expressions he's never given
4. c. cocaine
5. c. his name

1. In *Rocky Mountain High,* what has John Denver seen it rain ?
    a. fire in the sky ✓
    b. bullets from angry farmers ✓
    c. love from high above

2. According to Stevie Wonder in *Higher Ground,* while the people keep on dying, the powers keep on _____.
    a. thriving
    b. lying ✓ ✓
    c. testifying

3. In *Sunshine,* although the man says that in love and war all is fair, what does Jonathan Edwards add ?
    a. that war doesn't decide who's right, but only who's left
    b. that the man's a card-carrying Communist ✓
    c. that he's got cards he ain't showing ✓

4. In *Last Time I Saw Him,* how did Diana Ross's man leave ?
    a. by Greyhound Bus ✓ ✓
    b. by bicycle
    c. in a limousine

5. According to Reunion in *Life Is a Rock,* what lies at the end of their rainbow ?
    a. the greatest band that ever lived
    b. a rock & roll heaven ✓
    c. a golden oldie ✓

6. What has Michael Jackson *Got to Be There* to show his sweetheart ?
       a. that he's for real
       b. that he'll never leave her
       c. that she's his girl ✓

****

7. According to David Bowie in *Space Oddity*, what is the name of the astronaut ?
       a. Captain Kirk
       b. Major Tom ✓
       c. Sergeant Lowe

****

8. As Jim Croce is speaking with the *Operator*, with whom does he tell her that his ex-girlfriend is living ?
       a. with the operator's husband
       b. with his ex-friend Ray ✓
       c. with the bums on skid row

****

9. In *How Long*, Ace has his suspicions even though he adds that _____.
       a. he's not as dumb as he seems ✓
       b. he could never prove it in a court of law
       c. love has a funny way of playing games

****

10. In *Seasons In the Sun*, how long does Terry Jacks say he's known you ?
        a. not for very long
        b. since the age of nine or ten ✓
        c. for the better part of his childhood

11. What will Three Dog Night wash away with the rain in *Shambala* ?
    a. their trouble and pain ✓
    b. your perfume and lipstick
    c. their acne and lice

12. In *You're So Vain,* what does Carly Simon say you drove your Leer jet to Nova Scotia to see ?
    a. your mansion in the sky
    b. the passing of a crimson comet
    c. the total eclipse of the sun ✓

13. When do the Bee Gees say you can *Run to Me* ?
    a. when you're tired of running away
    b. when life starts getting you down
    c. when you need someone older ✓

14. According to Elton John, what is going to catch you when *The Bitch Is Back* ?
    a. the fever ✓
    b. her love
    c. the truth

15. In *Use Me Up,* what did Bill Withers tell his brother after being advised not to let you walk all over him ?
    a. that he was just a jealous man who didn't know a good thing when he saw it
    b. that love is a like a highway, and sometimes it's gonna get stepped on ✓
    c. that if he knew the truth, he'd wish he was in the same shoes ✓

16. In *Tell Me Something Good,* what does Rufus say is your problem ?
    a. you haven't been loved like you should ✓
    b. you're pretty and you know it only too well   ✓
    c. you can't say what's really on your mind

****

17. What does Barbra Streisand say is the only thing we will remember when we remember *The Way We Were* ?
    a. the memories   ✓
    b. the laughter ✓
    c. the one-night stands

****

18. According to Al Wilson in *Show and Tell,* what have you taken control of ?
    a. his soul ✓
    b. his heart   ✓
    c. his life

****

19. America says *I Need You* like a flower needs _____.
    a. the rain ✓   ✓
    b. a bee
    c. another flower

****

20. According to Carole King, what does her *Jazzman* do ?
    a. he makes her sing
    b. he takes her blues away ✓   ✓
    c. he takes her breath away

HARDER QUESTIONS: Worth 2 points each — 4 points if you can answer the question without the three choices !

****

1. In *Alone Again (Naturally)*, what does Gilbert O'Sullivan intend to do after he climbs to the top of the tower ?
   - a. gaze at the people below
   - b. jump off ✓
   - c. daydream

****

2. In *You and Me Against the World*, when does Helen Reddy say you can count on her ?
   - a. when you really need her
   - b. when the clouds of doubt come over you
   - c. when all the others turn their backs and walk away ✓

****

3. In *Draggin' the Line*, what does Tommy James suggest hugging when you're near ?
   - a. your sweetheart
   - b. a tree ✓
   - c. your mom

****

4. When everything is finished, how does Van Morrison say you'll be living with all your *Blue Money* ?
   - a. in clover ✓
   - b. like Captain Bly
   - c. you'll be feeling blue

****

5. Where and when does Billy Paul say that *Me and Mrs. Jones* get together ?
   - a. at the lunchroom during lunch and ten-minute breaks
   - b. at the same cafe, every day at 6:30 ✓
   - c. anywhere in those stolen moments when she can slip away

ANSWERS

***

1. a. fire in the sky
2. b. lying
3. c. that he's got cards he ain't showing
4. a. by Greyhound Bus
5. c. a golden oldie
6. c. that she's his girl
7. b. Major Tom
8. b. with his ex-friend Ray
9. a. he's not as dumb as he seems
10. b. since the age of nine or ten
11. a. their trouble and pain
12. c. the total eclipse of the sun
13. c. when you need someone older
14. a. the fever
15. c. that if he knew the truth, he'd wish he was in the same shoes
16. a. you haven't been loved like you should
17. b. the laughter
18. a. his soul
19. a. the rain
20. b. he takes her blues away

***

HARDER QUESTIONS--Answers

1. b. jump off
2. c. when all the others turn their backs and walk away
3. b. a tree
4. a. in clover
5. b. at the same cafe, every day at 6:30

1. According to Elton John, the *Candle In the Wind* burned out long before what really did ?
    a. the legend ✓
    b. the wick
    c. his love for you

2. Because Barry White *Can't Get Enough of Your Love, Babe,* what happens the more you give ?
    a. the more he wants ✓
    b. the less there is left
    c. the happier he is

3. In *Changes,* what does David Bowie tell today's rock & rollers?
    a. that they've still got the beat
    b. that as things change, things still remain the same
    c. that pretty soon they're gonna get older ✓

4. In *For the Love of Money,* the O'Jays nickname money _____.
    a. the fancy stuff you can't get enough
    b. the mean green ✓
    c. cash to dash

5. In *If You're Ready Come Go With Me,* what do the Staple Singers say is the only transportation you'll need ?
    a. faith
    b. your boogie shoes
    c. love ✓

6. In *Drift Away,* where does Dobie Gray want to get lost in ?
   - a. your love
   - b. your rock & roll ✓
   - c. his thoughts

   ✓

****

7. Because you don't call her anymore, what does Aretha Franklin say she's going to do *Until You Come Back to Me* ?
   - a. spread rumors and get you fired from your job
   - b. write you letters until you reply
   - c. rap on your door and tap on your window pane ✓

   ✓

****

8. Where does Gordon Lightfoot caution *Sundown* to beware if she's found there ?
   - a. in his best friend's house ✓
   - ✓ b. at his back stairs
   - c. on the beach at sunset

   ✗

****

9. In *Don't Go Breaking My Heart,* what does Elton John & Kiki Dee say they were when they were down ?
   - a. your clown ✓
   - b. your rising tide
   - c. your closest friend

   ✓

****

10. Because *Tonight's the Night (Gonna Be Alright),* what does Rod Stewart want to do for you ?
    - a. be your man
    - b. pour you a drink ✓
    - c. dress up as a clown

    ✓

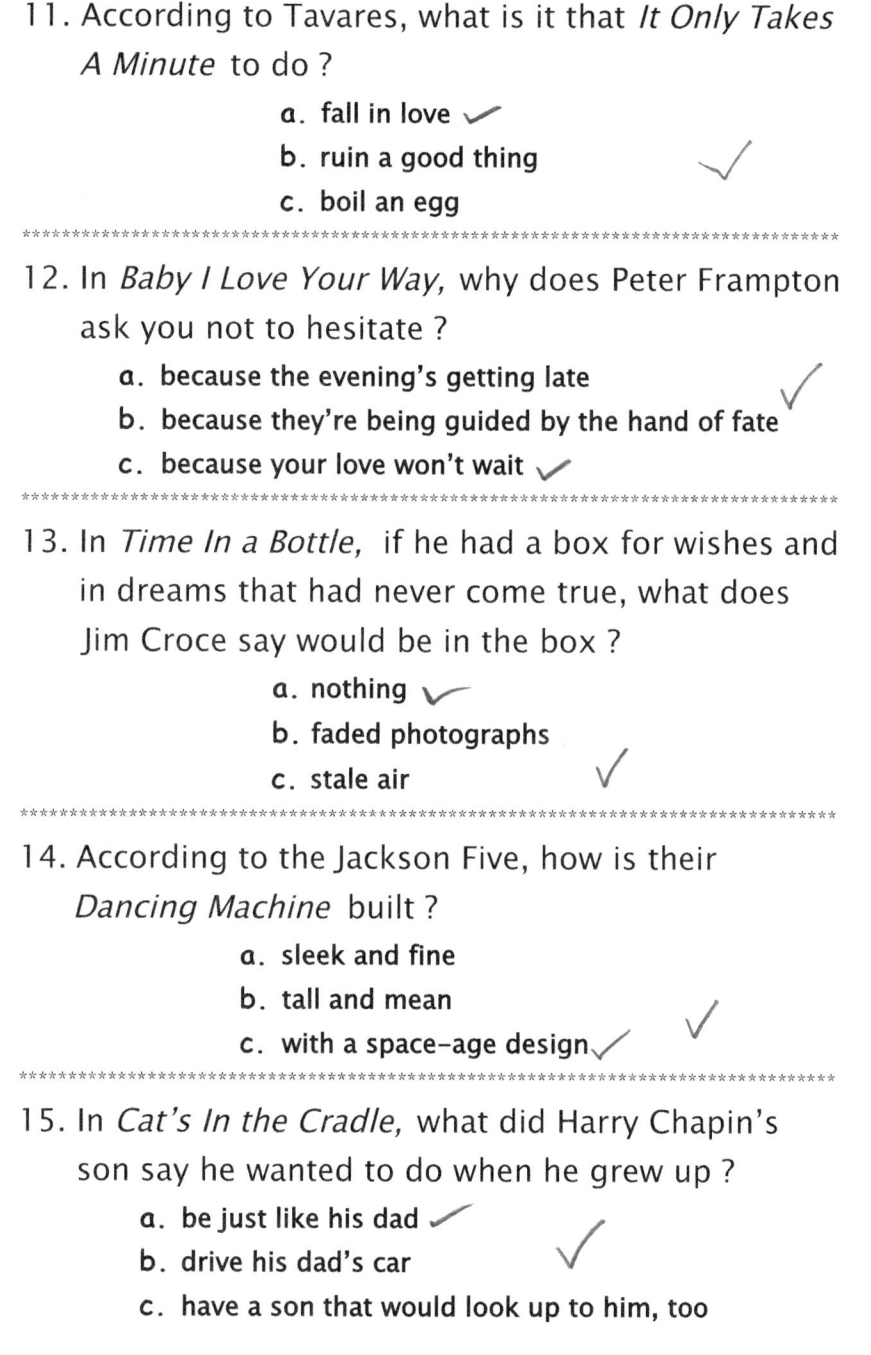

11. According to Tavares, what is it that *It Only Takes A Minute* to do ?
    a. fall in love ✓
    b. ruin a good thing   ✓
    c. boil an egg

***

12. In *Baby I Love Your Way,* why does Peter Frampton ask you not to hesitate ?
    a. because the evening's getting late   ✓
    b. because they're being guided by the hand of fate
    c. because your love won't wait ✓

***

13. In *Time In a Bottle,* if he had a box for wishes and in dreams that had never come true, what does Jim Croce say would be in the box ?
    a. nothing ✓
    b. faded photographs
    c. stale air   ✓

***

14. According to the Jackson Five, how is their *Dancing Machine* built ?
    a. sleek and fine
    b. tall and mean   ✓
    c. with a space-age design ✓

***

15. In *Cat's In the Cradle,* what did Harry Chapin's son say he wanted to do when he grew up ?
    a. be just like his dad ✓   ✓
    b. drive his dad's car
    c. have a son that would look up to him, too

16. What is Glen Campbell, the *Rhinestone Cowboy*, getting from people he doesn't even know?
    a. marriage proposals
    b. angry stares ✓
    c. letters ✓

17. In *50 Ways to Leave Your Lover*, what does Paul Simon tell Jack to do?
    a. slip out the back ✓ ✓
    b. step on a crack
    c. get your money back

18. According to Elton John in *Bennie and the Jets*, what did Bennie have?
    a. electric boots and a mohair suit ✓ ✓
    b. groupies and fan clubs
    c. hair flowing like angel wings

19. What is Linda Ronstadt going to do for a *Long Long Time*?
    a. cry
    b. hide in her dreams ✓ ✗
    ✓ c. love you

20. What does Paul McCartney have to say about what others call *Silly Love Songs*?
    a. they sure sell a lot of records
    b. what's wrong with that ✓ ✓
    c. there's nothing silly about love

HARDER QUESTIONS: Worth 2 points each — 4 points if you can answer the question without the three choices !

****

1. According to Helen Reddy, what does *Delta Dawn* walk downtown carrying ?
   - a. a suitcase ✓
   - b. her baby
   - c. nothing but an empty heart ✓

****

2. How tall is Elton John's *Island Girl* ?
   - a. 4' 11"
   - b. 5' 5" ✓
   - c. 6' 3" ✓

****

3. In Something Better to Do, what does Olivia Newton-John say she's lost somewhere on the shelf?
   - a. your telephone number
   - b. the key to your heart
   - c. her sense of humor ✓ ✓

****

4. In *Castles In the Air,* what does Don McLean say that castle walls lead him to ?
   - a. your heart
   - b. despair ✓ ✓
   - c. heaven on earth

****

5. What does Stevie Wonder say about *Superstition* ?
   - a. it rules the land
   - b. it makes people act strange ✓
   - c. it isn't the way ✓

ANSWERS

****

1. a. the legend
2. a. the more he wants
3. c. that pretty soon they're gonna get older
4. b. the mean green
5. c. love
6. b. your rock & roll
7. c. rap on your door and tap on your window pane
8. b. at his back stairs
9. a. your clown
10. b. pour you a drink
11. a. fall in love
12. c. because your love won't wait
13. a. nothing
14. c. with a space-age design
15. a. be just like his dad
16. c. letters
17. a. slip out the back
18. a. electric boots and a mohair suit
19. c. love you
20. b. what's wrong with that

****

HARDER QUESTIONS--Answers

1. b. a suitcase
2. c. 6' 3"
3. c. her sense of humor
4. b. despair
5. c. it isn't the way

1. Now that Eric Carmen is *All By Myself,* what does he say is gone ?
    a. all his worries and his fears ✓
    b. all the memories of his joy and happiness
    c. those days in which he made love just for fun ✗

2. In *The Night the Lights Went Out in Georgia,* who does Vicki Lawrence say you shouldn't trust ?
    a. the electrician
    b. a Southern lawyer
    c. a two-timing cowboy ✓   ✗

3. According to Natalie Cole, what is it that *This Will Be* ?
    a. her last goodbye ✓
    b. an everlasting love
    c. a wish come true   ✗

4. In *Philadelphia Freedom,* what did Elton John do on the day he was born ?
    a. he cried
    b. he swore he'd get out of this town
    c. he waved the flag ✓   ✓

5. Because *She's Gone,* who do Daryl Hall & John Oates say they'd pay to replace her ?
    a. the hooker down the street
    b. the almighty Lord above
    c. the devil ✓   ✓

6. What does Diana Ross say about any cure for her *Love Hangover*?
   - a. she should have had it yesterday ✓
   - b. she doesn't want it
   - c. it's in your kiss   ✗

****

7. What does Phoebe Snow say the *Poetry Man* does?
   - a. he makes things all right ✓
   - b. he talks in rhymes
   - c. he makes promises he can't keep   ✓

****

8. In *When Will I Be Loved,* what happens every time Linda Ronstadt meets a new love?
   - a. he breaks her heart in two ✓   ✓
   - b. she feels the same electric spark rush through her heart
   - c. she adds another notch to her belt

****

9. In *Love Machine,* who do the Miracles say they want to work for?
   - a. Uncle Sam
   - b. Venus, the goddess of love   ✓
   - c. nobody but you ✓

****

10. In *Show Me the Way,* what is the only thing that Peter Frampton can relate to?
    - a. the sea
    - b. the heartaches ✓   ✗
    - c. the lonely stars in the sky

11. In *You Sexy Thing*, what does Hot Chocolate believe in?
    a. miracles ✓
    b. hot love
    c. the power of persuasion

12. In *Turn the Beat Around*, what does Vicki Sue Robinson love to hear?
    a. words of love
    b. percussion ✓
    c. your name

13. What does Gary Wright believe that the *Dream Weaver* can help him reach?
    a. stardom
    b. the next level of happiness
    c. the morning light ✓

14. What is the only thing that Neil Sedaka says *Bad Blood* will do?
    a. leave a permanent scar
    b. mess up a good man's mind ✓
    c. fight with a bad Crip

15. KC & the Sunshine Band say *That's the Way (I Like It)* when you tell them what?
    a. that they're your lovin' man ✓
    b. that you want to dance all night
    c. that you're staying with them tonight

16. In *Best of My Love,* what did the Eagles say they were wasting their time with ?
    a. promises of a future that could never come to pass ✓
    b. disco music
    c. cheap talk and wine ✓

17. According to Grand Funk, what was it a *Bad Time* to do?
    a. be in love
    b. act like a fool ✓
    c. walk away from you ✗

18. According to Lynyrd Skynyrd, what will the *Free Bird* never do ?
    a. leave
    b. be caged
    c. change ✓ ✓

19. In *Golden Years,* David Bowie says that the nights are warm and the days are _____.
    a. young
    b. cool ✓ ✗
    c. hot

20. What do Earth, Wind & Fire say will happen when you wish upon a *Shining Star* ?
    a. the dream will take you very far
    b. you'll wake up in the morning with a gleam in your eye ✓
    c. you'll find that the star is gone tomorrow ✗

HARDER QUESTIONS: Worth 2 points each — 4 points if you can answer the question without the three choices !

****

1. In *They Just Can't Stop It The (Games People Play)*, what time was it when the Spinners were headed for the subway to go home ?
    a. 12:45
    b. 4:30
    c. 8:30 ✓   ✗

****

2. In *You're Sixteen*, when does Ringo Starr say you two fell in love ?
    a. when you'd just turned sixteen ✓
    b. on the night you two met
    c. when you were only six   ✗

****

3. How does Carl Douglas describe *Kung Fu Fighting* ?
    a. as judo on steroids
    b. as the latest dance craze ✓
    c. as an ancient Chinese art   ✗

****

4. In *Fallin' in Love,* what do Hamilton, Joe Frank & Reynolds say it seemed like they did just yesterday ?
    a. they made up with you
    b. they made love for the first time
    c. they met you ✓   ✗

****

5. Paul Anka says that because *(You're) Having My Baby*, what does this tell him ?
    a. that you'll be his forever ✓
    b. that you forgot to take the pill   ✗
    c. how much you love him

ANSWERS

****

1. c. those days in which he made love just for fun
2. b. a Southern lawyer
3. b. an everlasting love
4. c. he waved the flag
5. c. the devil
6. b. she doesn't want it
7. a. he makes things all right
8. a. he breaks her heart in two
9. c. nobody but you
10. a. the sea
11. a. miracles
12. b. percussion
13. c. the morning light
14. b. mess up a good man's mind
15. a. that they're your lovin' man
16. c. cheap talk and wine
17. a. be in love
18. c. change
19. a. young
20. a. the dream will take you very far

****

HARDER QUESTIONS--Answers

1. a. 12:45
2. b. on the night you two met
3. c. as an ancient Chinese art
4. b. they made love for the first time
5. c. how much you love him

1. What does John Lennon say about *Whatever Gets You Thru the Night*?
    a. it's good enough for him
    b. it may not be what he's got in mind
    c. it's alright

2. What does Heatwave say about the *Boogie Nights*?
    a. they're the best in town
    b. they're hot
    c. they're not as warm as the boogie days

3. In *Take It to the Limit,* what do the Eagles say they've always been?
    a. a gambler
    b. a dreamer
    c. a speed-freak

4. In *You Make Lovin' Fun,* what does Fleetwood Mac feel it's time to do if you believe in miracles?
    a. let the lovin' start
    b. give them a try
    c. share them with the world

5. In *Take the Money and Run,* who are the two young lovers the Steve Miller Band is singing about?
    a. Jack and Diane
    b. Billy Joe and Bobbie Sue
    c. Johnny and Billie Jean

6. What happens to Dan Hill *Sometimes When We Touch*?
   a. he's left with bruises
   b. he finds himself more in love with you
   c. he closes his eyes

7. Although she is here and warm for Bob Welch, what does he say would happen to his *Sentimental Lady* if he looked away?
   a. she would follow him
   b. she'd be cold to him
   c. she'd be gone

8. What is Jimmy Buffett doing in *Margaritaville*?
   a. sipping on a beer
   b. wasting away
   c. showing off his new tattoo

9. In *Don't Leave Me This Way*, what does Thelma Houston say she can't do without your love?
   a. dream
   b. plan a future with you
   c. survive

10. Where is Eddie Money keeping his *Two Tickets to Paradise*?
    a. in his pocket
    b. in a bank vault
    c. with the key to all his dreams

11. When A Taste of Honey says that you are no exception in *Boogie Oogie Oogie*, what do they say you've got to do just like everyone else?
    a. be cool
    b. boogie on the floor
    c. take it like a man

12. In *I Love the Night Life*, what doesn't Alicia Bridges want you to talk about tonight?
    a. love
    b. leaving
    c. your wife

13. In *An Everlasting Love*, what did Andy Gibb know even before he first held you tight in his arms?
    a. that you were made for him
    b. that he was losing you
    c. that you would be his first love

14. Under what conditions does Gloria Gaynor say *I Will Survive*?
    a. if you love her
    b. if the stars no longer shine
    c. without you by her side

15. In *Fool (If You Think It's Over)*, what does Chris Rea say to save for the day?
    a. your crying
    b. the sunshine
    c. your nighttime excuses

16. Jackson Browne is *Runnin' On Empty* and also runnin' _____.
    a. behind
    b. out of luck
    c. away

17. In *Escape (The Pina Colada Song)*, when Rupert Holmes answered the personal ad, who did he discover the woman was ?
    a. an undercover cop
    b. his own lady
    c. a man in disguise

18. When does Peter Brown say you should *Dance With Me* ?
    a. when they play the music tight
    b. now and forever
    c. when you're through dancing with all the other guys

19. Alan O'Day's *Undercover Angel* is his _____.
    a. live-in lover
    b. devil in disguise
    c. midnight fantasy

20. Where does KC & the Sunshine Band say you should *(Shake, Shake, Shake) Shake Your Booty* ?
    a. outside their doorstep
    b. on the dance floor
    c. anywhere you want

HARDER QUESTIONS: Worth 2 points each — 4 points if you can answer the question without the three choices !

****

1. Although they've got dancin' feet in *The Groove Line*, what does Heatwave say they don't have there ?
    - a. issues and hangups
    - b. a closing time
    - c. seats

****

2. During what month was it that Al Stewart felt himself go drifting into *Time Passages* ?
    - a. July
    - b. December
    - c. March

****

3. McFadden & Whitehead say that there *Ain't No Stoppin' Us Now* because they're _____.
    - a. polishing up their act
    - b. not giving up
    - c. so close to the top

****

4. In *Rhiannon (Will You Ever Win)*, Fleetwood Mac says she is like a cat in the dark and then she is _____.
    - a. a lion
    - b. a mousetrap
    - c. the darkness

****

5. Because others can dig his chains, what do the Village People say you can call the *Macho Man* ?
    - a. Mr. Ego
    - b. Mr. Cool
    - c. Mr. Macho

ANSWERS

****

1. c. it's alright
2. a. they're the best in town
3. b. a dreamer
4. b. give them a try
5. b. Billy Joe and Bobbie Sue
6. c. he closes his eyes
7. c. she'd be gone
8. b. wasting away
9. c. survive
10. a. in his pocket
11. b. boogie on the floor
12. a. love
13. b. that he was losing you
14. c. without you by her side
15. a. your crying
16. a. behind
17. b. his own lady
18. a. when they play the music tight
19. c. midnight fantasy
20. b. on the dance floor

****

HARDER QUESTIONS--Answers

1. c. seats
2. b. December
3. a. polishing up their act
4. c. the darkness
5. a. Mr. Ego

1. Although you may never become a rich man at the *Car Wash,* what does Rose Royce say it's better than doing ?
    a. being a bum
    b. shining shoes
    c. digging a ditch

2. Because these are the *Good Times,* what does Chic say to do ?
    a. forget about all the false promises
    b. leave your cares behind
    c. look ahead and enjoy the moment

3. What does Michael Johnson say is going to be *Bluer Than Blue* ?
    a. life without you
    b. tomorrow's sunshiny day
    c. the place where you kicked him

4. According to Gerry Rafferty in *Baker Street,* the city has so many people but was does it lack ?
    a. sunshine
    b. proper shelter for the homeless
    c. soul

5. According to Daryl Hall & John Oates, what can the *Rich Girl* rely on ?
    a. the old man's money
    b. all her money-loving friends
    c. the stock market

6. In *Swingtown,* what does the Steve Miller Band say they've been doing?
   - a. working so hard
   - b. listening to the music
   - c. rocking the place all night long

****

7. According to Donna Summer, the *Last Dance* is her last chance that night for _____.
   - a. being free
   - b. romance
   - c. having fun

****

8. In *Life's Been Good,* although Joe Walsh's Mazerati can do 185 m.p.h., what does he add?
   - a. it's out of gas
   - b. he lost his license, so he doesn't drive
   - c. there's no place to drive it anymore

****

9. According to Eddie Money in *Baby Hold On,* what has mama always told you ?
   - a. that there are too many fish in the sea
   - b. that money can't buy you love
   - c. that you should brush after every meal

****

10. In *Only the Good Die Young,* who does Billy Joel say he hangs around with?
    - a. a dangerous crowd
    - b. a rock and roll band
    - c. over-sexed women and under-sexed girls

11. According to Nicolette Larson, what is it going to take a *Lotta Love* to do ?
    a. find the right mate
    b. make her happy
    c. change the way things are

****

12. In *Shake Your Groove Thing,* what do Peaches & Herb want to show the world ?
    a. that dreams really can come true
    b. that their love is real
    c. that they can dance

****

13. According to Sylvester, when is it that *You Make Me Feel (Mighty Real)* ?
    a. when you're walking down the street with him
    b. when you're both on the dance floor
    c. when he wakes up in the morning

****

14. Where does Hot say the *Angel in Your Arms* is going to be tonight ?
    a. in the arms of someone else
    b. deep in your heart
    c. in your midnight fantasy

****

15. In *Sharing the Night Together,* what does Dr. Hook ask if you'd like ?
    a. a Tootsie Roll
    b. to slip away into the night
    c. someone new to talk to

16. In *Hot Stuff,* what is Donna Summer eating?
   a. she hasn't eaten anything since she met you
   b. she's eating her heart out
   c. she's eating chili burritos

****

17. Yvonne Elliman says that *If I Can't Have You,* who will she want?
   a. your little brother
   b. anyone who'll dance with her
   c. nobody

****

18. What do Earth, Wind & Fire find when they start to dance in *Boogie Wonderland*?
   a. peace of mind
   b. romance
   c. a way to express themselves

****

19. According to Chic, what is *Le Freak*?
   a. a French psychopath
   b. a new dance craze
   c. their boyfriend's new nickname

****

20. In *Sir Duke,* what does Stevie Wonder say you can do?
   a. feel it all over
   b. dance all night long
   c. make him beg like a dog

HARDER QUESTIONS: Worth 2 points each — 4 points if you can answer the question without the three choices!

****

1. Because he's found *Heaven On the 7th Floor*, what does Paul Nicholas not want you to do?
    - a. rescue him
    - b. bring him down
    - c. say goodbye

****

2. Rod Stewart says *The First Cut Is the Deepest* when it comes to doing what?
    - a. falling in love
    - b. trying to get to the front of the line
    - c. saying goodbye

****

3. According to Foxy in *Get Off*, what makes a lady find out what she wants in a man?
    - a. danger and excitement
    - b. a special kiss
    - c. jealousy and desire

****

4. In *Couldn't Get It Right*, what did Climax Blues Band hit the road to do?
    - a. look for you
    - b. start a concert tour
    - c. search for a better way

****

5. What word does Brick use to describe their *Dusic*?
    - a. hot
    - b. proper
    - c. funky

ANSWERS

****

1. c. digging a ditch
2. b. leave your cares behind
3. a. life without you
4. c. soul
5. a. the old man's money
6. a. working so hard
7. b. romance
8. b. he lost his license, so he doesn't drive
9. b. that money can't buy you love
10. a. a dangerous crowd
11. c. change the way things are
12. c. that they can dance
13. b. when you're both on the dance floor
14. a. in the arms of someone else
15. c. someone new to talk to
16. b. she's eating her heart out
17. c. nobody
18. b. romance
19. b. a new dance craze
20. a. feel it all over

****

HARDER QUESTIONS--Answers

1. a. rescue him
2. a. falling in love
3. a. danger and excitement
4. c. search for a better way
5. a. hot

1. In *Two Out of Three Ain't Bad,* what does Meat Loaf say about talking all night?
   - a. that it isn't going to get them anywhere
   - b. that it'll lead them to the truth
   - c. that it's a good way to stay awake

2. According to Frankie Valli, *Grease* is a word that's ---------------.
   - a. got a groove
   - b. hard to handle
   - c. got a new beat

3. Because they're a *Dirty White Boy,* what does Foreigner say they might ruin?
   - a. your good looks
   - b. your self-respect
   - c. your reputation

4. In *Hopelessly Devoted to You,* what does Olivia Newton-John say you think of her?
   - a. that she's just a girl who lives next door
   - b. that she's a fool who's willing to wait
   - c. that she's an angel who has come to the rescue

5. In what color is Nick Gilder's *Hot Child In the City* dressed?
   - a. fluorescent green
   - b. shocking pink
   - c. black

6. In *Right Down the Line*, what does Gerry Rafferty say you've been to him?
   a. as constant as the Northern Star
   b. as solid as the Rock of Gibraltar
   c. as annoying as a blood-thirsty mosquito

****

7. Where does Andy Gibb want to do his *Shadow Dancing*?
   a. under the moonlight
   b. across the floor
   c. anywhere he's alone

****

8. In *New Kid in Town*, what do the Eagles say about how your old friends treat you?
   a. they treat you like you're something new
   b. they don't even remember your name
   c. they treat you just fine

****

9. According to England Dan & John Ford Coley, what is that *It's Sad to Belong* to?
   a. a club that will accept them as a member
   b. a team filled with losers
   c. someone else when the right one comes along

****

10. In *We Are Family*, who does Sister Sledge say she has with her?
    a. all her friends
    b. only her lonely self
    c. all her sisters

11. At the *Y.M.C.A.*, the Village People say you can find many ways to _____.
　　　　a. fall in love
　　　　b. lose your pride
　　　　c. have a good time

12. What does Supertramp want you to *Give a Little Bit* of to them?
　　　　a. sympathy
　　　　b. your love
　　　　c. your attention

13. Because she's *Torn Between Two Lovers*, how does Mary MacGregor feel?
　　　　a. like a fool
　　　　b. like a hamburger between two buns
　　　　c. like a motherless child

14. In *Shame*, where does Evelyn "Champagne" King say she wants to be?
　　　　a. wrapped in your arms
　　　　b. on a desert island with you
　　　　c. in a ring filled with mud

15. According to the Bee Gees, what is *Tragedy*?
　　　　a. being locked in a love affair you can't escape from
　　　　b. realizing that you're just another Romeo
　　　　c. when the feeling's gone and you can't go on

16. In *Lay Down Sally,* what does Eric Clapton say there's nothing wrong with wanting him to do?
    a. become a movie star
    b. have you stay there with him
    c. make love to you

17. Because the feeling's right and the music's tight, what does GQ recommend for you to do in *Disco Nights (Rock Freak)*?
    a. get up
    b. find a dance partner
    c. light up

18. In *Head First,* how did you look when the Babys saw you for the first time?
    a. like an angel in white
    b. like a million bucks
    c. down-and-out

19. What does Melissa Manchester suggest instead when she says *Don't Cry Out Loud*?
    a. keep it inside
    b. keep your mouth shut
    c. save it for a rainy day

20. In *I Want Your Love,* what is it that Chic asks if you've ever wanted to try to see how well it fits?
    a. how well your answers fit to their questions
    b. how well their love fits
    c. how well their clothes fit

HARDER QUESTIONS: Worth 2 points each — 4 points if you can answer the question without the three choices!

****

1. In *Pop Muzik*, what does **M** suggest you boogie with?

   a. a mannequin
   b. a broom
   c. a suitcase

****

2. In *Jungle Love*, where did the Steve Miller Band meet you?

   a. on somebody's island
   b. on the dance floor
   c. in a back-street alley

****

3. In *Come Monday*, how many days did Jimmy Buffett spend in a brown L.A. Haze?

   a. two
   b. four
   c. twenty-four

****

4. According to Neil Diamond, how old was *Desiree*?

   a. seventeen
   b. nearly half his age
   c. almost twice his age

****

5. In *Da Doo Ron Ron*, what was the name of the girl that Shaun Cassidy met?

   a. Sue
   b. Jill
   c. Dawn

ANSWERS

****

1. a. that it isn't going to get them anywhere
2. a. got a groove
3. c. your reputation
4. b. that she's a fool who's willing to wait
5. c. black
6. a. as constant as the Northern Star
7. b. across the floor
8. a. they treat you like you're something new
9. c. someone else when the right one comes along
10. c. all her sisters
11. c. have a good time
12. b. your love
13. a. like a fool
14. a. wrapped in your arms
15. c. when the feeling's gone and you can't go on
16. b. have you stay there with him
17. a. get up
18. c. down-and-out
19. a. keep it inside
20. b. how well their love fits

****

HARDER QUESTIONS--Answers

1. c. a suitcase
2. a. on somebody's island
3. b. four
4. c. almost twice his age
5. b. Jill

ROCK TITLES QUESTIONS

If you're brave enough to test your skills,
here's a simple SCORING CHART:

(questions are worth 1 point each — "Harder Questions" are worth 2 points each . . . If you are able to identify the song without referring to the three choices, you receive twice the point value!)

If you score . . .

25+ Points: You probably STILL think it's 1975!
(Check your wardrobe!)

20-24: You probably paid more attention to
rock & roll than books & school!
(Check your report card!)

15-19: There's a lot of rock & roll memories
in your blood!
*(But maybe it's time to buy
a few more rock & roll CDs
& put on your boogie shoes!)*

10-14: Don't you wish you'd listened more closely
to rock & roll?!
(It's never too late to be hip!)

0-9: Where were YOU when rock began to rule?!
*(Time to get experienced —
run to your music store now!!!)*

(note: all answers are derived from lyrics within the song)

1. He wants to know if he can *have one more with you.*
    a. American Pie/Don McLean
    b. Photograph/Ringo Starr
    c. Moondance/Van Morrison

****

2. *If* their *backs should ever be against the wall,* they'll *be together — together you and I.*
    a. He Ain't Heavy, He's My Brother/Hollies
    b. I'll Be There/Jackson Five
    c. United We Stand/Brotherhood of Man

****

3. *You've got to have a friend in Jesus.*
    a. Jesus Is Just Alright/Byrds
    b. One Toke Over The Line/Brewer & Shipley
    c. Spirit In the Sky/Norman Greenbaum

****

4. Before them was every kind of girl — *long ones, tall ones, short ones, brown ones, black ones, big ones* . . .
    a. Going In Circles/Friends of Distinction
    b. 5-10-15-20 (25-30 Years of Love)/Presidents
    c. Spill the Wine/Eric Burdon & War

****

5. They *hold* their *pillow to* their *head and spring up in* their *bed screaming out the words* they *dread.*
    a. Hi-De-Ho/Blood, Sweat & Tears
    b. I Think I Love You/Partridge Family
    c. It's a Shame/Spinners

6. Now he's *freed from your spell,* and all he can do is *wish you well.*
   - a. Go Away Little Girl/Donny Osmond
   - b. Morning Has Broken/Cat Stevens
   - c. The Thrill Is Gone/B.B. King

****

7. They enjoy *sharing horizons that are near to* them, *watching the signs along the way.*
   - a. Signs/Five Man Electrical Band
   - b. We've Only Just Begun/Carpenters
   - c. Never Ending Song of Love/Delaney & Bonnie & Friends

****

8. He just wants to hear *some rhythm and blues music on the radio.*
   - a. Domino/Van Morrison
   - b. Chick-A-Boom/Daddy Dewdrop
   - c. Ain't No Sunshine/Bill Withers

****

9. *One glance was all it took, but now it's much too late for* them *to take a second look.*
   - a. I Want You Back/Jackson Five
   - b. Love On a Two-Way Street/Moments
   - c. Make It With You/Bread

****

10. He's *done a lot of foolish things that* he *really didn't mean.*
    - a. Signed Sealed Delivered I'm Yours/Stevie Wonder
    - b. I (Who Have Nothing)/Tom Jones
    - c. Easy Come, Easy Go/Bobby Sherman

11. Soon their tears *will be falling like rain.*
    a. How Can You Mend a Broken Heart/Bee Gees
    b. (I Know) I'm Losing You/Rare Earth
    c. Here Comes That Rainy Day Feeling Again/Fortunes

****

12. She's a *child of nature* and *friend of man.*
    a. Green-Eyed Lady/Sugarloaf
    b. Sweet Hitchhiker/Creedence Clearwater Revival
    c. Sweet City Woman/Stampeders

****

13. *Children playing in the park* don't know that they're *alone in the dark.*
    a. Have You Seen Her/Chi-Lites
    b. Make Me Smile/Chicago
    c. Slippin' Into Darkness/War

****

14. They *love you so much and* they *can't let go.*
    a. Tighter, Tighter/Alive & Kicking
    b. My Baby Loves Lovin'/White Plains
    c. Two Divided By Love/Grass Roots

****

15. He can hear *the music playing* and *your body swaying.*
    a. Heaven Help Us All/Stevie Wonder
    b. Knock Three Times/Tony Orlando & Dawn
    c. Oye Como Va/Santana

16. *The road is long with many a winding turn.*
     a. Help Me Make It Through the Night/Sammi Smith
     b. He Ain't Heavy, He's My Brother/Hollies
     c. The Long and Winding Road/Beatles

****

17. It's *coming down in three-part harmony.*
     a. An Old-Fashioned Love Song/Three Dog Night
     b. Jingle Jangle/Archies
     c. The Bells/Originals

****

18. *Who do you think you are?*
     a. Gypsy Woman/Brian Hyland
     b. Mr. Big Stuff/Jean Knight
     c. Express Yourself/Charles Wright & the Watts 103rd Street Rhythm Band

****

19. *Good morning, Mr. Sunshine — you brighten up their day.*
     a. Everybody Is a Star/Sly & the Family Stone
     b. In the Summertime/Mungo Jerry
     c. Lonely Days/Bee Gees

****

20. *Whenever they're asked what makes* their *dreams real,* they tell them that you do.
     a. Get Ready/Rare Earth
     b. Whole Lotta Love/Led Zeppelin
     c. Brown Sugar/Rolling Stones

HARDER QUESTIONS: Worth 2 points each — 4 points if you can NAME THAT TUNE without the three choices !

****

1. He *told you back in '52 that* he *would never go with you.*
    - a. Look What You Done For Me/Al Green
    - b. I Hear You Knocking/Dave Edmunds
    - c. It Don't Come Easy/Ringo Starr

****

2. They'll *fly to the East and fly to the West* — there'll be no place they can't call their own.
    - a. Free Ride/Edgar Winter Group
    - b. I'll Take You There/Staple Singers
    - c. One Fine Morning/Lighthouse

****

3. *He danced for those at minstrel shows and county fairs throughout the south.*
    - a. Amos Moses/Jerry Reed
    - b. Mr. Bojangles/Nitty Gritty Dirt Band
    - c. Superstar/Murray Head

****

4. They see *tin soldiers and Nixon coming.*
    - a. Peace Train/Cat Stevens
    - b. One Tin Soldier/Coven
    - c. Ohio/Crosby, Stills, Nash & Young

****

5. They wish they could sing how they feel, but *mostly* they're *silent.*
    - a. Look What They've Done to My Song Ma/New Seekers
    - b. Still Water (Love)/Four Tops
    - c. Beginnings/Chicago

ANSWERS

****

1. c. Moondance/Van Morrison
2. c. United We Stand/Brotherhood of Man
3. c. Spirit In the Sky/Norman Greenbaum
4. c. Spill the Wine/Eric Burdon & War
5. b. I Think I Love You/Partridge Family
6. c. The Thrill Is Gone/B.B. King
7. b. We've Only Just Begun/Carpenters
8. a. Domino/Van Morrison
9. a. I Want You Back/Jackson Five
10. a. Signed Sealed Delivered I'm Yours/Stevie Wonder
11. c. Here Comes That Rainy Day Feeling Again/Fortunes
12. a. Green-Eyed Lady/Sugarloaf
13. b. Make Me Smile/Chicago
14. a. Tighter, Tighter/Alive & Kicking
15. b. Knock Three Times/Tony Orlando & Dawn
16. b. He Ain't Heavy, He's My Brother/Hollies
17. a. An Old-Fashioned Love Song/Three Dog Night
18. b. Mr. Big Stuff/Jean Knight
19. c. Lonely Days/Bee Gees
20. a. Get Ready/Rare Earth

****

HARDER QUESTIONS--Answers

1. b. I Hear You Knocking/Dave Edmunds
2. c. One Fine Morning/Lighthouse
3. b. Mr. Bojangles/Nitty Gritty Dirt Band
4. c. Ohio/Crosby, Stills, Nash & Young
5. c. Beginnings/Chicago

1. *Loneliness is such a sad affair.*
    a. I Need You/America
    b. One/Three Dog Night
    c. Superstar/Carpenters

****

2. They wonder why *a picture paints a thousand words and yet* they *can't paint you.*
    a. If/Bread
    b. Reflections of My Life/Marmalade
    c. You Are Everything/Stylistics

****

3. *Different strokes for different folks.*
    a. 25 or 6 to 4/Chicago
    b. Lola/Kinks
    c. Thank You (Falettinme Be Mice Elf Agin)/Sly & the Family Stone

****

4. *When Jesus walked, he washed our sins away.*
    a. Spirit In the Sky/Norman Greenbaum
    b. Oh Happy Day/Edwin Hawkins Singers
    c. Put Your Hand In the Hand/Ocean

****

5. They *don't know where to look for love,* and they *just don't know how.*
    a. Oh Girl/Chi-Lites
    b. O-o-h Child/Five Stairsteps
    c. Where Is the Love/Roberta Flack & Donny Hathaway

6. The *three men* he admired most *caught the last train for the coast.*
    a. Take Me Home, Country Roads/John Denver
    b. American Pie/Don McLean
    c. Where Do the Children Play/Cat Stevens

****

7. *There's a girl in the harbor town* who *serves sailors whiskey and wine.*
    a. Honky Tonk Women/Rolling Stones
    b. Brandy/Looking Glass
    c. Sweet Mary/Wadsworth Mansion

****

8. They claim to be *a lovable man who can take you to the nearest star.*
    a. Roundabout/Yes
    b. All Right Now/Free
    c. Vehicle/Ides of March

****

9. She whispered that it *feels so right* being with them tonight.
    a. Layla/Derek & the Dominoes
    b. Go All the Way/Raspberries
    c. Sylvia's Mother/Dr. Hook

****

10. They got along *making each other cry without ever knowing why.*
    a. Hurting Each Other/Carpenters
    b. Here Comes That Rainy Day Feeling Again/Fortunes
    c. How Can You Mend a Broken Heart/Bee Gees

11. If they *couldn't find* their *way back home, it just wouldn't be fair.*
    a. Precious and Few/Climax
    b. Everything I Own/Bread
    c. If I Could Reach You/5th Dimension

****

12. Even though there's that same unhappy feeling — *a dizzy hangup* — they still never want to let you go.
    a. I Just Want to Celebrate/Rare Earth
    b. Don't Pull Your Love/Hamilton, Joe Frank & Reynolds
    c. Never Can Say Goodbye/Jackson Five

****

13. *The new day will dawn for those who stand long, and the forest will echo with laughter.*
    a. Riders On the Storm/Doors
    b. What Is Life/George Harrison
    c. Stairway to Heaven/Led Zeppelin

****

14. *You better hurry 'cause it's going fast.*
    a. Share the Land/Guess Who
    b. Come and Get It/Badfinger
    c. Come and Get Your Love/Redbone

****

15. *We ought to live together.*
    a. Share the Land/Guess Who
    b. United We Stand/Brotherhood of Man
    c. Black & White/Three Dog Night

16. *As* they *were walking down the street one day, a man came up to* them *and asked* them *what the time was that was on* their *watch.*
   a. Too Late to Turn Back Now/Cornelius Brothers & Sister Rose
   b. Does Anybody Really Know What Time It Is/Chicago
   c. Reflections of My Life/Marmalade

****

17. She wonders *"does anyone stay in one place anymore?"*
   a. So Far Away/Carole King
   b. Brand New Key/Melanie
   c. That's the Way I've Always Heard It Should Be/Carly Simon

****

18. As he goes through his life, he'll *wish for her all the sweet things she can find.*
   a. The Air That I Breathe/Hollies
   b. Best of My Love/Eagles
   c. Diary/Bread

****

19. They'd *rather live in his world than live without him* in theirs.
   a. When Will I See You Again/Three Degrees
   b. Goodbye to Love/Carpenters
   c. Midnight Train to Georgia/Gladys Knight & the Pips

****

20. They're *sewn together, like a hand in glove.*
   a. Ain't No Woman (Like The One I've Got)/Four Tops
   b. I'm Stone In Love With You/Stylistics
   c. Skin Tight/Ohio Players

HARDER QUESTIONS: Worth 2 points each — 4 points if you can NAME THAT TUNE without the three choices !
****

1. There's *evolution, revolution, gun control, the sound of soul.*
    a. Gimme Some Truth/John Lennon
    b. Ball of Confusion/Temptations
    c. Space Race/Billy Preston

****

2. They remember that they *were flying low and hit something in the air.*
    a. D.O.A./Bloodrock
    b. Something In the Air/Thunderclap Newman
    c. 25 or 6 to 4/Chicago

****

3. *Blood's thicker than the mud.*
    a. Family Affair/Sly & the Family Stone
    b. Mama's Pearl/Jackson Five
    c. Freddie's Dead/Curtis Mayfield

****

4. He is *sitting on a park bench eyeing little girls with evil intent.*
    a. Evil Ways/Santana
    b. The Rapper/Jaggerz
    c. Aqualung/Jethro Tull

****

5. *Go ahead and hate your neighbor* because you can *justify it in the end.*
    a. Isn't It a Pity/George Harrison
    b. One Tin Soldier/Coven
    c. Bring the Boys Home/Freda Payne

ANSWERS

****

1. c. Superstar/Carpenters
2. a. If/Bread
3. c. Thank You (Falettinme Be Mice Elf Agin)/Sly & the Family Stone
4. b. Oh Happy Day/Edwin Hawkins Singers
5. a. Oh Girl/Chi-Lites
6. b. American Pie/Don McLean
7. b. Brandy/Looking Glass
8. c. Vehicle/Ides of March
9. b. Go All the Way/Raspberries
10. a. Hurting Each Other/Carpenters
11. a. Precious and Few/Climax
12. c. Never Can Say Goodbye/Jackson Five
13. c. Stairway to Heaven/Led Zeppelin
14. b. Come and Get It/Badfinger
15. a. Share the Land/Guess Who
16. b. Does Anybody Really Know What Time It Is/Chicago
17. a. So Far Away/Carole King
18. c. Diary/Bread
19. c. Midnight Train to Georgia/Gladys Knight & the Pips
20. a. Ain't No Woman (Like The One I've Got)/Four Tops

****

HARDER QUESTIONS--Answers

1. b. Ball of Confusion/Temptations
2. a. D.O.A./Bloodrock
3. a. Family Affair/Sly & the Family Stone
4. c. Aqualung/Jethro Tull
5. b. One Tin Soldier/Coven

1. They're *everywhere — blocking out the scenery.*
    a. Hot Pants/James Brown
    b. Signs/Five Man Electrical Band
    c. Fire and Rain/James Taylor

****

2. *You should have heard her just around midnight.*
    a. Cracklin' Rosie/Neil Diamond
    b. Lola/Kinks
    c. Brown Sugar/Rolling Stones

****

3. They've got this and it's *the morning in May.*
    a. Money/Pink Floyd
    b. Rainy Days and Mondays/Carpenters
    c. Pieces of April/Three Dog Night

****

4. He's *a picker, a grinner, a lover, and a sinner.*
    a. Jazzman/Carole King
    b. The Bitch Is Back/Elton John
    c. The Joker/Steve Miller Band

****

5. Frank Zappa & the Mothers of Invention were at the best place around until someone *with a flare gun burned it to the ground.*
    a. Higher Ground/Stevie Wonder
    b. Smoke On the Water/Deep Purple
    c. Rock On/David Essex

6. They *remember finding out about you.*
    a. Day After Day/Badfinger
    b. Pay to the Piper/Chairmen Of The Board
    c. No Time/Guess Who

****

7. If people stare, *just let them burn their eyes on you moving.*
    a. Hold Your Head Up/Argent
    b. Bang a Gong (Get It On)/T. Rex
    c. The Show Must Go On/Three Dog Night

****

8. Day after day, they must *face the world of strangers* where they don't belong.
    a. I Won't Last a Day Without You/Carpenters
    b. You and Me Against the World/Helen Reddy
    c. Back Stabbers/O'Jays

****

9. *They'll all be there together when they meet in one big show.*
    a. Rock & Roll Heaven/Righteous Brothers
    b. Sweet Home Alabama/Lynyrd Skynyrd
    c. Hollywood Swinging/Kool & the Gang

****

10. Without you, *life has no meaning or rhyme,* as if *notes to a song out of time.*
    a. Just Don't Want to Be Lonely/Main Ingredient
    b. You're a Special Part of Me/Marvin Gaye & Diana Ross
    c. You Make Me Feel Brand New/Stylistics

11. *We don't have tomorrow, but we had yesterday.*
    a. Touch Me In the Morning/Diana Ross
    b. The Way Were/Barbra Streisand
    c. Why Can't We Live Together/Tommy Thomas

****

12. They wonder if you're *stowing away the time.*
    a. Reeling In the Years/Steely Dan
    b. Whatever Gets You Thru the Night/John Lennon & the Plastic Ono Band
    c. Touch a Hand (Make a Friend)/Staple Singers

****

13. The only wish on their mind is that *tomorrow will be the same for you and* them.
    a. Top of the World/Carpenters
    b. Just You 'n' Me/Chicago
    c. My Love/Paul McCartney & Wings

****

14. He's got a *Nikon* camera to take his photographs.
    a. Keep On Smilin'/Wet Willie
    b. Kodachrome/Paul Simon
    c. Photograph/Ringo Starr

****

15. They like the *country morning, all covered in dew* — she's got a way *to make a man feel shiny and new.*
    a. Little Bitty Pretty One/Jackson Five
    b. Sweet City Woman/Stampeders
    c. Long Cool Woman (In a Black Dress)/Hollies

16. They *never thought that fairytales came true — but they come true* when they're near you.
    a. Betcha By Golly, Wow/Stylistics
    b. Shambala/Three Dog Night
    c. Layla/Derek & the Dominoes

****

17. They *lay awake and watched until the morning light washed away the darkness of the lonely night.*
    a. It's Going to Take Some Time/Carpenters
    b. (Last Night) I Didn't Get to Sleep at All/5th Dimension
    c. The Love I Lost/Harold Melvin & the Blue Notes

****

18. *Madame Onassis* has got *nothing on you.*
    a. Sweet and Innocent/Donny Osmond
    b. You Wear It Well/Rod Stewart
    c. You're So Vain/Carly Simon

****

19. *Tell all the folks in Egypt and Israel* not to miss this because if you do, they'll *feel sorry for you.*
    a. Long Train Running/Doobie Brothers
    b. Masterpiece/Temptations
    c. Love Train/O'Jays

****

20. *They say Spain is pretty.*
    a. Never Been to Spain/Three Dog Night
    b. Space Oddity/David Bowie
    c. Daniel/Elton John

HARDER QUESTIONS: Worth 2 points each — 4 points if you can NAME THAT TUNE without the three choices !

****

1. Meeting you was their destiny — *heaven made you specially.*
    - a. Top of the World/Carpenters
    - b. Could Be I'm Falling In Love/Spinners
    - c. Me and Baby Brother/War

****

2. *No one knows what it's like to be hated, to be fated to telling only lies.*
    - a. Behind Blue Eyes/Who
    - b. Ain't No Sunshine/Bill Withers
    - c. Inner City Blues/Marvin Gaye

****

3. All they want to do is *see you smiling, too,* hoping that maybe once in their life they'll *be making love to you.*
    - a. Pretty Lady/Lighthouse
    - b. Wildflower/Skylark
    - c. Heartbeat—It's a Lovebeat/DeFranco Family

****

4. He's *been down one time, and* he's *been down two times.*
    - a. Alone Again (Naturally)/Gilbert O'Sullivan
    - b. Last Song/Edward Bear
    - c. Drowning In the Sea of Love/Joe Simon

****

5. *This is* their *fork in the road — there's nowhere to go.*
    - a. Slippin' Into Darkness/War
    - b. I'll Be Around/Spinners
    - c. I'll Meet You Halfway/Partridge Family

ANSWERS

****

1. b. Signs/Five Man Electrical Band
2. c. Brown Sugar/Rolling Stones
3. c. Pieces of April/Three Dog Night
4. c. The Joker/Steve Miller Band
5. b. Smoke On the Water/Deep Purple
6. a. Day After Day/Badfinger
7. a. Hold Your Head Up/Argent
8. a. I Won't Last a Day Without You/Carpenters
9. a. Rock & Roll Heaven/Righteous Brothers
10. c. You Make Me Feel Brand New/Stylistics
11. a. Touch Me In the Morning/Diana Ross
12. a. Reeling In the Years/Steely Dan
13. a. Top of the World/Carpenters
14. b. Kodachrome/Paul Simon
15. b. Sweet City Woman/Stampeders
16. a. Betcha By Golly, Wow/Stylistics
17. b. (Last Night) I Didn't Get to Sleep at All/5th Dimension
18. b. You Wear It Well/Rod Stewart
19. c. Love Train/O'Jays
20. c. Daniel/Elton John

****

HARDER QUESTIONS--Answers

1. b. Could Be I'm Falling In Love/Spinners
2. a. Behind Blue Eyes/Who
3. a. Pretty Lady/Lighthouse
4. c. Drowning In the Sea of Love/Joe Simon
5. b. I'll Be Around/Spinners

1. Now they realize that *love's not all that it's supposed to be.*
    a. Everybody Plays the Fool/Main Ingredient
    b. Feelin' Stronger Every Day/Chicago
    c. You Little Trustmaker/Tymes

****

2. *You led* him *away from home* because *you didn't want to be alone.*
    a. Maggie May/Rod Stewart
    b. Goodbye Yellow Brick Road/Elton John
    c. Rikki Don't Lose That Number/Steely Dan

****

3. *It's a supernatural delight.*
    a. Nights In White Satin/Moody Blues
    b. Morning Has Broken/Cat Stevens
    c. Dancing In the Moonlight/King Harvest

****

4. Each face that they see *brings back memories of being with you.*
    a. The Tears of a Clown/Smokey Robinson & the Miracles
    b. Precious and Few/Climax
    c. You Are Everything/Stylistics

****

5. *The days surround your daylight there.*
    a. Ventura Highway/America
    b. I Saw the Light/Todd Rundgren
    c. It Never Rains In Southern California/Albert Hammond

6. *The outlaws had* them *pinned down at the fort.*
   - a. The Night Chicago Died/Paper Lace
   - b. I Shot the Sheriff/Eric Clapton
   - c. The Cisco Kid/War

****

7. *Ain't no difference if you're black or white.*
   - a. Brother Louie/Stories
   - b. Black and White/Three Dog Night
   - c. Don't Expect Me to Be Your Friend/Lobo

****

8. *When he goes to sleep at night, you're always a part of his dreams.*
   - a. You're Sixteen/Ringo Starr
   - b. I'll Have to Say I Love You In a Song/Jim Croce
   - c. I Can Help/Billy Swan

****

9. *Wherever he laid his hat was his home; and when he died, all he left* them *was alone.*
   - a. Living In the Past/Jethro Tull
   - b. Papa Was a Rolling Stone/Temptations
   - c. A Cowboy's Work Is Never Done/Sonny & Cher

****

10. When you and they meet, *it's a good sensation.*
    - a. Heartbeat—It's a Lovebeat/DeFranco Family
    - b. Double Lovin'/Osmonds
    - c. I Think I Love You/Partridge Family

11. A man was *selling ice cream and singing Italian songs.*
    a. Joy to the World/Three Dog Night
    b. Saturday In the Park/Chicago
    c. Crocodile Rock/Elton John

****

12. It will *only cost you fifty cents* to see *what life has done to those like you and me.*
    a. Sha La La (Make Me Happy)/Al Green
    b. Life Is a Rock (But the Radio Rolled Me)/Reunion
    c. Sideshow/Blue Magic

****

13. Still she's glad for what you and she had and how she *once loved you.*
    a. Stoney End/Barbra Streisand
    b. It's Too Late/Carole King
    c. Rose Garden/Lynn Anderson

****

14. If they were a businessman, they'd *be so successful that* they'd *scare Wall Street to death.*
    a. I've Got to Use My Imagination/Gladys Knight & the Pips
    b. Takin' Care of Business/Bachman-Turner Overdrive
    c. I'm Stone In Love With You/Stylistics

****

15. *Hooga-Shaka.*
    a. The Streak/Ray Stevens
    b. Hooked On a Feeling/Blue Swede
    c. Earache My Eye/Cheech & Chong

16. They *headed out for Las Vegas* but *only made it out to Needles.*
    a. Never Been to Spain/Three Dog Night
    b. Lonely Days/Bee Gees
    c. (Last Night) I Didn't Get to Sleep at All/5th Dimension

****

17. He *doesn't have much money,* but if he did, he'd *buy a big house* where you two could both live.
    a. Black Magic Woman/Santana
    b. Your Song/Elton John
    c. Clair/Gilbert O'Sullivan

****

18. *The county judge who held a grudge will search forevermore.*
    a. Band On the Run/Paul McCartney & Wings
    b. Fox On the Run/Sweet
    c. Free Bird/Lynyrd Skynyrd

****

19. *Woman, take* him *in your arms.*
    a. Rock Me Gently/Andy Kim
    b. Lookin' For a Love/Bobby Womack
    c. Rock Your Baby/George McCrae

****

20. *Don't give up until you drink from the silver cup.*
    a. Be Thankful For What You've Got/William DeVaughn
    b. Lonely People/America
    c. Shining Star/Earth, Wind & Fire

HARDER QUESTIONS: Worth 2 points each — 4 points if you can NAME THAT TUNE without the three choices !
****

1. His dad said *"Son, you're gonna drive me to drinkin'"*.
   a. Rockin' Pneumonia & the Boogie Woogie Flu/Johnny Rivers
   b. Indiana Wants Me/R. Dean Taylor
   c. Hot Rod Lincoln/Commander Cody & His Lost Planet Airmen

****

2. Although others advise them not to *waste your time,* they don't feel that they're wasting their time, and anyway, it's their time.
   a. You're Still A Young Man/Tower of Power
   b. If I Could Reach You/5th Dimension
   c. Lookin' Through the Eyes of Love/Partridge Family

****

3. *It's sad to think* that they're *not gonna make it.*
   a. Sad Sweet Dreamer/Sweet Sensations
   b. Neither One of Us (Wants to Be the First to Say Goodbye)/ Gladys Knight & the Pips
   c. Must of Got Lost/J. Geils Band

****

4. They want this to be done *in perfect harmony.*
   a. Never Ending Song of Love/Delaney & Bonnie & Friends
   b. I'd Like to Teach the World to Sing/Hillside Singers
   c. An Old-Fashioned Love Song/Three Dog Night

****

5. *Love runs deeper than any ocean — it clouds your mind with emotion.*
   a. Break Up to Make Up/Stylistics
   b. Song Sung Blue/Neil Diamond
   c. Everybody Plays the Fool/Main Ingredient

ANSWERS

****

1. b. Feelin' Stronger Every Day/Chicago
2. a. Maggie May/Rod Stewart
3. c. Dancing In the Moonlight/King Harvest
4. c. You Are Everything/Stylistics
5. a. Ventura Highway/America
6. c. The Cisco Kid/War
7. a. Brother Louie/Stories
8. c. I Can Help/Billy Swan
9. b. Papa Was a Rolling Stone/Temptations
10. a. Heartbeat—It's a Lovebeat/DeFranco Family
11. b. Saturday In the Park/Chicago
12. c. Sideshow/Blue Magic
13. b. It's Too Late/Carole King
14. c. I'm Stone In Love With You/Stylistics
15. b. Hooked On a Feeling/Blue Swede
16. a. Never Been to Spain/Three Dog Night
17. b. Your Song/Elton John
18. a. Band On the Run/Paul McCartney & Wings
19. c. Rock Your Baby/George McCrae
20. b. Lonely People/America

****

HARDER QUESTIONS--Answers

1. c. Hot Rod Lincoln/Commander Cody & His Lost Planet Airmen
2. a. You're Still A Young Man/Tower of Power
3. b. Neither One of Us (Wants to Be the First to Say Goodbye)/Gladys Knight & the Pips
4. b. I'd Like to Teach the World to Sing/Hillside Singers
5. c. Everybody Plays the Fool/Main Ingredient

1. *Don't you feel it growing day by day ?*
    a. Bang a Gong (Get It On)/T. Rex
    b. Listen to the Music/Doobie Brothers
    c. Power of Love/Joe Simon

****

2. Sometimes he thinks *it's a sin* when he feels *like he's winning* when he's losing again.
    a. Knockin' On Heaven's Door/Bob Dylan
    b. Sundown/Gordon Lightfoot
    c. Rock On/David Essex

****

3. *Tonight's the night we always knew it would feel so right.*
    a. Stay With Me/Faces
    b. Betcha By Golly, Wow/Stylistics
    c. I Wanna Be With You/Raspberries

****

4. She makes them *feel like a river.*
    a. My Woman From Tokyo/Deep Purple
    b. Thinkin' of You/Loggins & Messina
    c. Brandy/Looking Glass

****

5. *You sure do shine.*
    a. Natural High/Bloodstone
    b. Sunshine On My Shoulders/John Denver
    c. Diamond Girl/Seals & Crofts

6. They know *it won't let them down* because they're *already standing on the ground.*
    a. Peaceful Easy Feeling/Eagles
    b. My Love/Paul McCartney & Wings
    c. Feelin' Stronger Every Day/Chicago

****

7. *It's coming from* her *heart and not* her *head.*
    a. Feel Like Makin' Love/Roberta Flack
    b. A Love Song/Anne Murray
    c. I Honestly Love You/Olivia Newton-John

****

8. They were *out on the road for forty days.*
    a. We're An American Band/Grand Funk
    b. Bennie & the Jets/Elton John
    c. Sweet Home Alabama/Lynyrd Skynyrd

****

9. In the *land of milk and honey,* you must put the cards *on the table.*
    a. Goodtime Charlie's Got the Blues/Danny O'Keefe
    b. Do It Again/Steely Dan
    c. Ramblin' Man/Allman Brothers Band

****

10. Their love is *like a ship on the ocean.*
    a. Jungle Boogie/Kool & the Gang
    b. Rock the Boat/Hues Corporation
    c. Take Me In Your Arms (Rock Me)/Doobie Brothers

11. He was *a consecrated boy singing in the Sunday choir.*
    a. Loves Me Like a Rock/Paul Simon
    b. I'm Just a Singer (In a Rock 'n' Roll Band)/Moody Blues
    c. Oh Very Young/Cat Stevens

****

12. Every time he tried to tell you he loved you, *the words just came out wrong.*
    a. Be Thankful For What You've Got/William DeVaughn
    b. I'll Have to Say I Love You In a Song/Jim Croce
    c. Oh My My/Ringo Starr

****

13. They ask you to *send it off in a letter to yourself.*
    a. We May Never Pass This Way Again/Seals & Crofts
    b. Don't Call Us We'll Call You/Sugarloaf
    c. Rikki Don't Lose That Number/Steely Dan

****

14. He *can hardly talk but he sure knows how to sing the blues.*
    a. My Girl Bill/Jim Stafford
    b. Rock 'n Roll Baby/Stylistics
    c. Beach Baby/First Class

****

15. *Now* they *know* their *life has meaning.*
    a. Fallin' In Love/Hamilton, Joe Frank & Reynolds
    b. You Little Trustmaker/Tymes
    c. (I've Been) Searchin' So Long/Chicago

16. It's traveling *down around the corner, half a mile from here.*
    a. Fox On the Run/Sweet
    b. Jet/Paul McCartney
    c. Long Train Runnin'/Doobie Brothers

****

17. *He calls his child Jesus because he likes the name.*
    a. Levon/Elton John
    b. The Joker/Steve Miller Band
    c. Rocky/Austin Roberts

****

18. *You'll soon discover* that it'll *sometimes make you weep and moan* as you *sit all day by the telephone.*
    a. A Very Special Love Song/Charlie Rich
    b. Mighty Love/Spinners
    c. Kung Fu Fighting/Carl Douglas

****

19. *You're fine and you're mine and you look so divine.*
    a. Come and Get Your Love/Redbone
    b. Hooked On a Feeling/Blue Swede
    c. You Ought to Be With Me/Al Green

****

20. They've *got to make the best of a bad situation.*
    a. Wishing You Were Here/Chicago
    b. It Only Takes a Minute/Tavares
    c. I've Got to Use My Imagination/Gladys Knight & the Pips

HARDER QUESTIONS: Worth 2 points each — 4 points if you can NAME THAT TUNE without the three choices !
****

1. Once *every boy and girl* was their friend, but in today's revolution people *don't know what they're fighting.*
    a. I'd Love to Change the World/Ten Years After
    b. Whatever Gets You Thru the Night/John Lennon & the Plastic Ono Band
    c. Living In the Past/Jethro Tull
****

2. *Suddenly they heard the sirens and everybody started to run.*
    a. The Night Chicago Died/Paper Lace
    b. Long Cool Woman (In a Black Dress)/Hollies
    c. The Night the Lights Went Out In Georgia/Vicki Lawrence
****

3. *Like a man said in his song, " help me make it through the night."*
    a. I Don't Like to Sleep Alone/Paul Anka
    b. Help Me Make It Through the Night/John Holt
    c. Before the Next Teardrop Falls/Freddy Fender
****

4. *Sleep's the only freedom that she knows.*
    a. Wildfire/Michael Murphey
    b. Pillow Talk/Sylvia
    c. Wildflower/Skylark
****

5. *You're built like a car* with a *hub cap diamond-star halo.*
    a. Bang a Gong (Get It On)/T. Rex
    b. One Helluva Woman/Mac Davis
    c. Hot Rod Lincoln/Commander Cody

ANSWERS

****

1. b. Listen to the Music/Doobie Brothers
2. b. Sundown/Gordon Lightfoot
3. c. I Wanna Be With You/Raspberries
4. a. My Woman From Tokyo/Deep Purple
5. c. Diamond Girl/Seals & Crofts
6. a. Peaceful Easy Feeling/Eagles
7. c. I Honestly Love You/Olivia Newton-John
8. a. We're An American Band/Grand Funk
9. b. Do It Again/Steely Dan
10. b. Rock the Boat/Hues Corporation
11. a. Loves Me Like a Rock/Paul Simon
12. b. I'll Have to Say I Love You In a Song/Jim Croce
13. c. Rikki Don't Lose That Number/Steely Dan
14. b. Rock 'n Roll Baby/Stylistics
15. c. (I've Been) Searchin' So Long/Chicago
16. c. Long Train Runnin'/Doobie Brothers
17. a. Levon/Elton John
18. b. Mighty Love/Spinners
19. a. Come and Get Your Love/Redbone
20. c. I've Got to Use My Imagination/Gladys Knight & the Pips

****

HARDER QUESTIONS--Answers

1. c. Living In the Past/Jethro Tull
2. b. Long Cool Woman (In a Black Dress)/Hollies
3. a. I Don't Like to Sleep Alone/Paul Anka
4. c. Wildflower/Skylark
5. a. Bang a Gong (Get It On)/T. Rex

1. She told them that they *need educatin' — gotta go to school.*
   a. Do It Baby/Miracles
   b. You Ain't Seen Nothin' Yet/Bachman-Turner Overdrive
   c. Witchy Woman/Eagles

****

2. He remembers *when rock was young* and he had *an old gold Chevy* and a place of his own.
   a. Mother and Child Reunion/Paul Simon
   b. American Pie/Don McLean
   c. Crocodile Rock/Elton John

****

3. He's *moving ahead so life won't pass* him *by.*
   a. All I Know/Art Garfunkel
   b. I Got a Name/Jim Croce
   c. Drowning In the Sea of Love/Joe Simon

****

4. *Night is calling* and they *are falling.*
   a. Dance With Me/Orleans
   b. Nights on Broadway/Bee Gees
   c. The Boys are Back In Town/Thin Lizzy

****

5. *Brother what a night it really was; brother what a fight it really was.*
   a. The Night Chicago Died/Paper Lace
   b. The Night the Lights Went Out In Georgia/Vicki Lawrence
   c. Right Place, Wrong Time/Dr. Hook

6. Loving you is *so damn easy.*
   a. Go All the Way/Raspberries
   b. Ain't No Woman (Like the One I've Got)/Four Tops
   c. Just You 'n' Me/Chicago

****

7. It's *blowing through the jasmine in* their *mind.*
   a. Dueling Banjos/Eric Weissberg & Steve Mandell
   b. Summer Breeze/Seals & Crofts
   c. Jungle Fever/Chakachas

****

8. They've *been driving all night* and their hands are wet on the wheel.
   a. Killer Queen/Queen
   b. Helen Wheels/Paul McCartney & Wings
   c. Radar Love/Golden Earring

****

9. He's *got to keep you pleased in every way* he *can — he's gonna give you all of* him *as much as you can stand.*
   a. Wedding Song/Paul Stookey
   b. Never, Never Gonna Give Ya Up/Barry White
   c. Burning Love/Elvis Presley

****

10. *Sometimes late when things are real and people share the gift of gab between themselves, some are quick to take the bait and catch the perfect prize that waits among the shelves.*
    a. Roundabout/Yes
    b. Tin Man/America
    c. Hold Your Head Up/Argent

11. *Listening to the teachers* just isn't their bag.
    a. Smokin' In the Boys Room/Brownsville Station
    b. Clap for the Wolfman/Guess Who
    c. Rock and Roll Music/Beach Boys

****

12. *Make it simple to last your whole life long*, and don't worry *that it's not good enough for anyone else to hear.*
    a. Play Me/Neil Diamond
    b. Sing/Carpenters
    c. A Love Song/Anne Murray

****

13. They'll *help you through the night.*
    a. We're An American Band/Grand Funk
    b. Call On Me/Chicago
    c. Who Loves You/Four Seasons

****

14. You can't plant him *in your penthouse;* he's *going back to* his *plow.*
    a. Goodbye Yellow Brick Road/Elton John
    b. Living for the City/Stevie Wonder
    c. Walk On the Wild Side/Lou Reed

****

15. *If* he *had a song that* he *could sing for you,* he'd *sing a song to make you feel this way.*
    a. My Melody of Love/Bobby Vinton
    b. Sunshine on My Shoulders/John Denver
    c. L–O–V–E/Al Green

16. *Before you leave* them behind, they want to *feel happy one more time.*
    - a. Take Me In Your Arms/Doobie Brothers
    - b. Do It ('Til You're Satisfied)/B.T. Express
    - c. Get Down Tonight/KC & the Sunshine Band

17. He wants you to *give* him *things that don't get lost, like a coin that won't get tossed.*
    - a. Speak to the Sky/Rick Springfield
    - b. Old Man/Neil Young
    - c. Time In a Bottle/Jim Croce

18. They don't know whether you and they are in love or are *just friends,* and whether it's *just the beginning* or if it's *the end.*
    - a. If You Want Me to Stay/Sly & the Family Stone
    - b. Diamond Girl/Seals & Crofts
    - c. When Will I See You Again/Three Degrees

19. *Daddy, please don't — it wasn't his fault.*
    - a. I'm Not Lisa/Jessi Colter
    - b. Midnight Blue/Melissa Manchester
    - c. Run Joey Run/David Geddes

20. He's *quit those days and* his *redneck ways.*
    - a. Superfly/Curtis Mayfield
    - b. Uneasy Rider/Charlie Daniels Band
    - c. Honky Cat/Elton John

HARDER QUESTIONS: Worth 2 points each — 4 points if you can NAME THAT TUNE without the three choices !

****

1. He's *gonna whip you on a natural high.*
   - a. Once You Get Started/Rufus
   - b. Let's Get It On/Marvin Gaye
   - c. Boogie Down/Eddie Kendricks

****

2. They'll *take to the sky,* loving you more until the day they die.
   - a. Natural High/Bloodstone
   - b. If I Could Reach You/5th Dimension
   - c. Radar Love/Golden Earring

****

3. They *couldn't escape if they wanted to.*
   - a. I Won't Last a Day Without You/Carpenters
   - b. Band On the Run/Paul McCartney & Wings
   - c. Waterloo/Abba

****

4. *It's the power of the Lone Star State.*
   - a. China Grove/Doobie Brothers
   - b. Americans/Byron MacGregor
   - c. Spiders and Snakes/Jim Stafford

****

5. Although you *hurt* them *to* their *soul*, they still feel with *every breath* and *every move* that they *can't let you go.*
   - a. Fight the Power/Isley Brothers
   - b. D'yer Maker/Led Zeppelin
   - c. Free Ride/Edgar Winter Group

ANSWERS

****

1. b. You Ain't Seen Nothin' Yet/Bachman-Turner Overdrive
2. c. Crocodile Rock/Elton John
3. b. I Got a Name/Jim Croce
4. a. Dance With Me/Orleans
5. a. The Night Chicago Died/Paper Lace
6. c. Just You 'n' Me/Chicago
7. b. Summer Breeze/Seals & Crofts
8. c. Radar Love/Golden Earring
9. b. Never, Never Gonna Give Ya Up/Barry White
10. b. Tin Man/America
11. a. Smokin' In the Boys Room/Brownsville Station
12. b. Sing/Carpenters
13. c. Who Loves You/Four Seasons
14. a. Goodbye Yellow Brick Road/Elton John
15. b. Sunshine on My Shoulders/John Denver
16. a. Take Me In Your Arms/Doobie Brothers
17. b. Old Man/Neil Young
18. c. When Will I See You Again/Three Degrees
19. c. Run Joey Run/David Geddes
20. c. Honky Cat/Elton John

****

HARDER QUESTIONS--Answers

1. c. Boogie Down/Eddie Kendricks
2. a. Natural High/Bloodstone
3. c. Waterloo/Abba
4. a. China Grove/Doobie Brothers
5. b. D'yer Maker/Led Zeppelin

1. They *picked up your vibes.*
    a. More, More, More/Andrea True Connection
    b. Miracles/Jefferson Starship
    c. Let Your Love Flow/Bellamy Brothers

****

2. *Soldier boy kisses girl — leaves behind a tragic world.*
    a. Listen to What the Man Said/Wings
    b. That's the Way of the World/Earth, Wind & Fire
    c. They Just Can't Stop It (The Games People Play)/Spinners

****

3. *Drive-in movies, comic books and blue jeans; Howdy Doody, baseball cards and birthdays.*
    a. Crocodile Rock/Elton John
    b. Seasons In the Sun/Terry Jacks
    c. Old Days/Chicago

****

4. *Big boys don't cry.*
    a. Who Do You Think You Are/Bo Donaldson & the Heywoods
    b. I'm Not In Love/10cc
    c. I Never Cry/Alice Cooper

****

5. Music *is the healing force of the world.*
    a. I Love Music/O'Jays
    b. Could It Be Magic/Barry Manilow
    c. Get Closer/Seals & Crofts

6. They've been *searching for the daughter of the devil himself* as well as for *an angel in white.*
   a. One of These Nights/Eagles
   b. Somebody to Love/Queen
   c. You Sexy Thing/Hot Chocolate

****

7. They did not think *a girl could be so cruel.*
   a. Jackie Blue/Ozark Mountain Daredevils
   b. My Old School/Steely Dan
   c. Third Rate Romance/Amazing Rhythm Aces

****

8. *Butterflies are free to fly, fly away.*
   a. Free Bird/Lynyrd Skynyrd
   b. She's Gone/Daryl Hall & John Oates
   c. Someone Saved My Life Tonight/Elton John

****

9. You woo them *until the sun comes up.*
   a. Say You Love Me/Fleetwood Mac
   b. Junior's Farm/Paul McCartney & Wings
   c. Jungle Love/Steve Miller Band

****

10. They're *gonna dance with* their *baby 'til the night is through.*
    a. Get Up and Boogie/Silver Convention
    b. (Shake, Shake, Shake) Shake Your Booty/KC & the Sunshine Band
    c. Saturday Night/Bay City Rollers

11. They're *floating like the heavens above.*
    a. Everlasting Love/Carl Carlton
    b. Rock & Roll Heaven/Righteous Brothers
    c. Muskrat Love/Captain & Tennille

***

12. You don't know them but they say *"I'm your brother".*
    a. Takin' It to the Streets/Doobie Brothers
    b. The Rubberband Man/Spinners
    c. (Don't Fear) The Reaper/Blue Öyster Cult

***

13. It *don't use no gas.*
    a. Low Rider/War
    b. Express/B.T. Express
    c. Chevy Van/Sammy Johns

***

14. They ask *how do you like your love ?*
    a. Tell Me Something Good/Rufus
    b. Come and Get Your Love/Redbone
    c. More, More, More/Andrea True Connection

***

15. *They knew all the right people — they took all the right pills; they threw outrageous parties,* and *they paid heavenly bills.*
    a Life In the Fast Lane/Eagles
    b. Dream On/Aerosmith
    c. Movin'/Brass Construction

16. His *heart's a virgin — it ain't never been tried.*
    a. Love Won't Let Me Wait/Major Harris
    b. I Never Cry/Alice Cooper
    c. I Want You/Marvin Gaye

17. There was *something in the air that night* and the stars were *shining for liberty.*
    a. Philadelphia Freedom/Elton John
    b. Wreck of the Edmund Fitzgerald/Gordon Lightfoot
    c. Fernando/Abba

18. They *dream of a girl they used to know* — they *close* their *eyes and she slips away.*
    a. Imaginary Lover/Atlanta Rhythm Section
    b. Kiss and Say Goodbye/Manhattans
    c. More Than a Feeling/Boston

19. They say that it's *very nice to know* that she *ain't got no place left to go.*
    a. If You Leave Me Now/Chicago
    b. That's the Way (I Like It)/KC & the Sunshine Company
    c. Evil Woman/Electric Light Orchestra

20. *When* they *think about you,* they *think about love.*
    a. For the Love of Money/O'Jays
    b. Feel Like Makin' Love/Bad Company
    c. Bungle In the Jungle/Jethro Tull

HARDER QUESTIONS: Worth 2 points each — 4 points if you can NAME THAT TUNE without the three choices !
****

1. She wants you to *light* her *heart with your everlasting flame.*
   - a. Rockin' Chair/Gwen McCrae
   - b. I'm a Woman/Maria Muldaur
   - c. Please Mr. Please/Olivia Newton-John

****

2. *In a blizzard he was lost.*
   - a. Fly Robin Fly/Silver Convention
   - b. Wildfire/Michael Murphey
   - c. Timothy/Buoys

****

3. *Your mood is like a circus wheel — you're changing all the time.*
   - a. Over My Head/Fleetwood Mac
   - b. Jive Talkin'/Bee Gees
   - c. Island Girl/Elton John

****

4. If you *show* them *a mountain so high,* they'll *show you love that'll last forever.*
   - a. Who Loves You/Four Seasons
   - b. With Your Love/Jefferson Starship
   - c. Sweet Love/Commodores

****

5. They've *never been awake* — they've *never seen a daybreak leaning on* their *pillow in the morning.*
   - a. Love Hurts/Nazareth
   - b. Magic/Pilot
   - c. Love Rollercoaster/Ohio Players

ANSWERS

****

1. b. Miracles/Jefferson Starship
2. a. Listen to What the Man Said/Wings
3. c. Old Days/Chicago
4. b. I'm Not In Love/10cc
5. a. I Love Music/O'Jays
6. a. One of These Nights/Eagles
7. b. My Old School/Steely Dan
8. c. Someone Saved My Life Tonight/Elton John
9. a. Say You Love Me/Fleetwood Mac
10. c. Saturday Night/Bay City Rollers
11. c. Muskrat Love/Captain & Tennille
12. a. Takin' It to the Streets/Doobie Brothers
13. a. Low Rider/War
14. c. More, More, More/Andrea True Connection
15. a. Life In the Fast Lane/Eagles
16. b. I Never Cry/Alice Cooper
17. c. Fernando/Abba
18. c. More Than a Feeling/Boston
19. c. Evil Woman/Electric Light Orchestra
20. b. Feel Like Makin' Love/Bad Company

****

HARDER QUESTIONS--Answers

1. a. Rockin' Chair/Gwen McCrae
2. b. Wildfire/Michael Murphey
3. a. Over My Head/Fleetwood Mac
4. c. Sweet Love/Commodores
5. b. Magic/Pilot

1. *The world was right when she made love to* them.
    a. Love So Right/Bee Gees
    b. Bad Time/Grand Funk
    c. Old Days/Chicago

****

2. They're *not ready for the altar* but they still feel that there's time when a woman *sure can be a friend* to them.
    a. That Lady/Isley Brothers
    b. Sister Golden Hair/America
    c. I'll Be Good to You/Brothers Johnson

****

3. They *didn't even know her name,* but they're *never gonna be the same.*
    a. Take It Easy/Eagles
    b. Can't Get It Out of My Head/Electric Light Orchestra
    c. December '63 (Oh What A Night)/Four Seasons

****

4. They saw your face *and that's the last they've seen of* their *heart.*
    a. You Are the Woman/Firefall
    b. Rhiannon (Will You Ever Win)/Fleetwood Mac
    c. Nights Are Forever Without You/England Dan & John Ford Coley

****

5. The *catfish are jumpin'.*
    a. Junk Food Junkie/Larry Groce
    b. If You Know What I Mean/Neil Diamond
    c. Black Water/Doobie Brothers

6. After all the years, they're *still having fun.*
       a. I Love Music/O'Jays
       b. Still The One/Orleans
       c. Maybe I'm Amazed/Wings

****

7. They sing that it's *my time of year.*
       a. December '63 (Oh What a Night)/Four Seasons
       b. Summer/War
       c. Feel Like Makin' Love/Bad Company

****

8. They've been *looking real hard* to *find a job,* but it just keeps getting tougher every day.
       a. Rock'n Me/Steve Miller Band
       b. My Little Town/Simon & Garfunkel
       c. Takin' It to the Streets/Doobie Brothers

****

9. *Friday night,* they'll be *dressed to kill.*
       a. Stayin' Alive/Bee Gees
       b. The Boys Are Back In Town/Thin Lizzy
       c. You and Me/Alice Cooper

****

10. *The Eastern moon is ready for a wet kiss to make the tide rise again.*
       a. Thank God I'm a Country Boy/John Denver
       b. Muskrat Love/Captain & Tennille
       c. Moonlight Feels Right/Starbuck

11. She's *young and sweet — only seventeen — having the time of* her *life.*
    a. Dancing Queen/Abba
    b. Shannon/Henry Gross
    c. Hey Deanie/Shaun Cassidy

****

12. *This whole world still looks the same — another frame.*
    a. Don't Call Us We'll Call You/Sugarloaf
    b. Tequila Sunrise/Eagles
    c. My Little Town/Simon & Garfunkel

****

13. *If you give a little more than you're asking for, your love will turn the key.*
    a. I Just Want To Be Your Everything/Andy Gibb
    b. Let 'Em In/Wings
    c. It's So Easy/Linda Ronstadt

****

14. *If you wake up and don't want to smile, open your eyes and look at the day — you'll see things in a different way.*
    a. Don't Stop/Fleetwood Mac
    b. Southern Nights/Glen Campbell
    c. Rock and Roll Music/Beach Boys

****

15. *Sailing away on the crest of a wave* is *like magic.*
    a. Magic/Pilot
    b. Fly Like an Eagle/Steve Miller Band
    c. Livin' Thing/Electric Light Orchestra

16. When they feel cold, you always warm them, and when they feel they can't go on, *you come and hold them.*
    a. Sky High/Jigsaw
    b. Just Don't Want to Be Lonely/Main Ingredient
    c. Sara Smile/Daryl Hall & John Oates

*****

17. They wonder if they're *rough enough* and *rich enough.*
    a. So In To You/Atlanta Rhythm Section
    b. I'm Your Boogie Man/KC & the Sunshine Band
    c. Beast of Burden/Rolling Stones

*****

18. They'll be *playing with the boys all night.*
    a. Beth/Kiss
    b. We Are the Champions/Queen
    c. We're an American Band/Grand Funk Railroad

*****

19. *Take it easy.*
    a. Hot Line/Sylvers
    b. Slow Ride/Foghat
    c. We're All Alone/Rita Coolidge

*****

20. He's *got chills* that *are multiplying* and he's *losing control* because the power you're supplying *is electrifying.*
    a. That's Rock 'n' Roll/Shaun Cassidy
    b. Heaven On the 7th Floor/Paul Nicholas
    c. You're the One That I Want/John Travolta & Olivia Newton-John

HARDER QUESTIONS: Worth 2 points each — 4 points if you can NAME THAT TUNE without the three choices!

****

1. He looks back on when he was *a little nappy-headed boy.*
   - a. I Wish/Stevie Wonder
   - b. I'm Easy/Keith Carradine
   - c. Only Sixteen/Dr. Hook

****

2. *Something she said has stuck in* his *head and* he *can't get away.*
   - a. Baby, I Love Your Way/Peter Frampton
   - b. Swearin' to God/Frankie Valli
   - c. Let Her In/John Travolta

****

3. *She came to* him *just like the morning sun.*
   - a. Ebony Eyes/Bob Welch
   - b. Desiree/Neil Diamond
   - c. My Angel Baby/Toby Beau

****

4. There's *no more standing outside the wall* because he's got himself *together and* he's *having a ball.*
   - a. You Make Me Feel Like Dancing/Leo Sayer
   - b. Got to Give It Up/Marvin Gaye
   - c. Love Is In the Air/John Paul Young

****

5. *When you put your arms around* them, they *feel so satisfied.*
   - a. Feels Like the First Time/Foreigner
   - b. Back In Love Again/L.T.D.
   - c. Don't Stop/Fleetwood Mac

ANSWERS

****

1. a. Love So Right/Bee Gees
2. b. Sister Golden Hair/America
3. c. December '63 (Oh What A Night)/Four Seasons
4. a. You Are the Woman/Firefall
5. c. Black Water/Doobie Brothers
6. b. Still The One/Orleans
7. b. Summer/War
8. a. Rock'n Me/Steve Miller Band
9. b. The Boys Are Back In Town/Thin Lizzy
10. c. Moonlight Feels Right/Starbuck
11. a. Dancing Queen/Abba
12. b. Tequila Sunrise/Eagles
13. a. I Just Want To Be Your Everything/Andy Gibb
14. a. Don't Stop/Fleetwood Mac
15. c. Livin' Thing/Electric Light Orchestra
16. c. Sara Smile/Daryl Hall & John Oates
17. c. Beast of Burden/Rolling Stones
18. a. Beth/Kiss
19. b. Slow Ride/Foghat
20. c. You're the One That I Want/John Travolta & Olivia Newton-John

****

HARDER QUESTIONS--Answers

1. a. I Wish/Stevie Wonder
2. c. Let Her In/John Travolta
3. b. Desiree/Neil Diamond
4. b. Got to Give It Up/Marvin Gaye
5. b. Back In Love Again/L.T.D.

1. They wonder why you *won't talk about the reasons why you and* they fight.
   a. After the Love Has Gone/Earth, Wind & Fire
   b. Head Games/Foreigner
   c. Smoke From a Distant Fire/Sanford-Townsend Band

2. He remembers *standing on the corner at midnight, trying to get* his *courage up.*
   a. On Broadway/George Benson
   b. Main Street/Bob Seger
   c. Thunder Island/Jay Ferguson

3. They *were searching on a one-way street;* they *were hoping for a chance to meet,* waiting *for the operator on the line.*
   a. Just Remember I Love You/Firefall
   b. Sweet Talkin' Woman/Electric Light Orchestra
   c. Take a Chance On Me/Abba

4. This is *the night of the expanding man.*
   a. Love Is Alive/Gary Wright
   b. Deacon Blues/Steely Dan
   c. A Little Bit More/Dr. Hook

5. *You don't have to prove to* her *that you're beautiful to strangers —* she *has lovin' eyes of* her *own.*
   a. You Belong to Me/Carly Simon
   b. Our Love/Natalie Cole
   c. I Just Fall In Love Again/Anne Murray

6. This time is for the *romantic lady, single baby, sophisticated mama, disco lady.*
   a. Special Lady/Ray, Goodman & Brown
   b. Shining Star/Manhattans
   c. Ladies Night/Kool & the Gang

****

7. *You're the light in* their *deepest, darkest hours — you're* their *savior when* they *fall.*
   a. Babe/Styx
   b. Love Is Like Oxygen/Sweet
   c. How Deep Is Your Love/Bee Gees

****

8. *Time keeps on slipping into the future.*
   a. Right Time of the Night/Jennifer Warnes
   b. Fly Like An Eagle/Steve Miller Band
   c. Used To Be My Girl/O'Jays

****

9. They want you to *try to understand the way* they *feel under your command.*
   a. Angel In Your Arms/Hot
   b. Because the Night/Patti Smith Group
   c. You Made Me Believe In Magic/Bay City Rollers

****

10. *It's all right once you get past the pain.*
    a. Love Will Find a Way/Pablo Cruise
    b. The Groove Line/Heatwave
    c. Love Takes Time/Orleans

11. They know *your plans don't include* them.
    a. Every Time I Think Of You/Babys
    b. We've Got Tonite/Bob Seger & the Silver Bullet Band
    c. I'm Not Gonna Let It Bother Me Tonight/Atlanta Rhythm Section

****

12. He was *a sentimental fool trying hard to recreate what had yet to be created.*
    a. What A Fool Believes/Doobie Brothers
    b. We Don't Talk Anymore/Cliff Richard
    c. I Can't Stand It No More/Peter Frampton

****

13. They say *it took so long just to realize* that they're much too strong to compromise.
    a. Biggest Part of Me/Ambrosia
    b. The Logical Song/Supertramp
    c. Don't Look Back/Boston

****

14. *By giving* her *all you've got, your love has captured* her.
    a. The Closer I Get to You/Roberta Flack & Donny Hathaway
    b. Nobody Does It Better/Carly Simon
    c. Last Dance/Donna Summer

****

15. *Some dance to remember, some dance to forget.*
    a. Shadow Dancing/Andy Gibb
    b. Hotel California/Eagles
    c. Runnin' on Empty/Jackson Browne

16. There's *no reason to pretend* — they *knew it had to end someday this way.*
    a. Telephone Line/Electric Light Orchestra
    b. Too Much, Too Little, Too Late/Johnny Mathis & Deniece Williams
    c. Best of My Love/Emotions

****

17. They *regret the moment that they let you go.*
    a. Happy Anniversary/Little River Band
    b. Tragedy/Bee Gees
    c. Reunited/Peaches & Herb

****

18. Their *mind is racing but* their *body is in the lead.*
    a. This Time I'm In It For Love/Player
    b. Hold the Line/Toto
    c. Double Vision/Foreigner

****

19. *Nobody wants to go home now — there's too much going on.*
    a. Heartache Tonight/Eagles
    b. I Love the Night Life/Alicia Bridges
    c. Too Much Heaven/Bee Gees

****

20. *Don't you worry because* they *know where they stand* — they *don't need this love;* they *don't need your hand.*
    a. Heartless/Heart
    b. Sail On/Commodores
    c. Minute by Minute/Doobie Brothers

HARDER QUESTIONS: Worth 2 points each — 4 points if you can NAME THAT TUNE without the three choices !
****

1. *So you think you're a Romeo playing a part in a picture show.*
    - a. Who Are You/Who
    - b. Hot Legs/Rod Stewart
    - c. Take the Long Way Home/Supertramp

****

2. *Just one touch from you and* they're *a slave.*
    - a. Every 1's A Winner/Hot Chocolate
    - b. Beast of Burden/Rolling Stones
    - c. Kiss You All Over/Exile

****

3. *Go-cart Mozart was checking out the weather charts to see if it was safe outside.*
    - a. Come Sail Away/Styx
    - b. Blinded By the Light/Manfred Mann's Earth Band
    - c. Life In the Fast Lane/Eagles

****

4. *Johnny, rosin up your bow and play your fiddle hard.*
    - a. Rock 'n' Roll Fantasy/Bad Company
    - b. Pilot of the Airwaves/Charlie Dore
    - c. The Devil Went Down to Georgia/Charlie Daniels Band

****

5. He's *walked along Saint Thomas beach* with you *a million times.*
    - a. I Like Dreamin'/Kenny Nolan
    - b. Weekend In New England/Barry Manilow
    - c. Just the Way You Are/Billy Joel

ANSWERS

****

1. b. Head Games/Foreigner
2. b. Main Street/Bob Seger
3. b. Sweet Talkin' Woman/Electric Light Orchestra
4. b. Deacon Blues/Steely Dan
5. a. You Belong to Me/Carly Simon
6. c. Ladies Night/Kool & the Gang
7. c. How Deep Is Your Love/Bee Gees
8. b. Fly Like An Eagle/Steve Miller Band
9. b. Because the Night/Patti Smith Group
10. a. Love Will Find a Way/Pablo Cruise
11. b. We've Got Tonite/Bob Seger & the Silver Bullet Band
12. a. What A Fool Believes/Doobie Brothers
13. c. Don't Look Back/Boston
14. a. The Closer I Get to You/Roberta Flack & Donny Hathaway
15. b. Hotel California/Eagles
16. b. Too Much, Too Little, Too Late/Johnny Mathis & Deniece Williams
17. c. Reunited/Peaches & Herb
18. c. Double Vision/Foreigner
19. a. Heartache Tonight/Eagles
20. c. Minute by Minute/Doobie Brothers

****

HARDER QUESTIONS--Answers

1. c. Take the Long Way Home/Supertramp
2. a. Every 1's A Winner/Hot Chocolate
3. b. Blinded By the Light/Manfred Mann's Earth Band
4. c. The Devil Went Down to Georgia/Charlie Daniels Band
5. a. I Like Dreamin'/Kenny Nolan

1. They'd *take her back, as a matter of fact.*
    a. Used To Be My Girl/O'Jays
    b. After the Love Has Gone/Earth, Wind & Fire
    c. Alive Again/Chicago

2. He *really has enjoyed* his *stay but* he *must be moving on.*
    a. Cheeseburger In Paradise/Jimmy Buffett
    b. On and On/Stephen Bishop
    c. Goodbye Stranger/Supertramp

3. *All that* he *so wants to give you* is *only a heartbeat away.*
    a. It's Ecstasy When You Lay Down Next To Me/Barry White
    b. Wonderful Tonight/Eric Clapton
    c. When I Need You/Leo Sayer

4. They've been *holding out so long* and *sleeping all alone.*
    a. Tragedy/Bee Gees
    b. Miss You/Rolling Stones
    c. Isn't It Time/Babys

5. *It's the hottest spot north of Havana.*
    a. Hot Child In the City/Nick Gilder
    b. Copacabana/Barry Manilow
    c. New York Groove/Ace Frehley

6. It's *like thunder and lightning the way your love is frightening.*
   - a. Cruel to Be Kind/Nick Lowe
   - b. I Just Wanna Stop/Gino Vannelli
   - c. Knock on Wood/Amii Stewart

****

7. *You fight the love you feel for* him *instead of giving in . . . but* he *can wait forever.*
   - a. You're In My Heart/Rod Stewart
   - b. Goodbye Girl/David Gates
   - c. Magnet and Steel/Walter Egan

****

8. *If you don't come home to her, there'll be nobody left in this world to hold* her *tight, nobody left in this world to kiss goodnight.*
   - a. Hopelessly Devoted To You/Olivia Newton-John
   - b. Ooh Baby Baby/Linda Ronstadt
   - c. Emotion/Samantha Sang

****

9. *He was a Midwestern boy on his own.*
   - a. Hollywood Nights/Bob Seger & the Silver Bullet Band
   - b. Time Passages/Al Stewart
   - c. Coward of the County/Kenny Rogers

****

10. *Don't blame it on the sunshine; don't blame it on the moonlight.*
    - a. I Go Crazy/Paul Davis
    - b. Blame It On The Boogie/Jacksons
    - c. We Just Disagree/Dave Mason

11. She begs you please not to *take your love from* her *because* she's *your forevermore, 'til eternity.*
    a. Heaven Knows/Donna Summer
    b. Come to Me/France Joli
    c. Heaven Must Have Sent You/Bonnie Pointer

12. They want to know if you'll *come upstairs* and *have a drink of champagne.*
    a. Just a Song Before I Go/Crosby, Stills & Nash
    b. What's Your Name/Lynyrd Skynyrd
    c. We've Got Tonite/Bob Seger & the Silver Bullet Band

13. You say that they waste their time, but they *can't get you off* their *mind* because they *can't let go.*
    a. Take a Chance On Me/Abba
    b. I Was Made For Lovin' You/Kiss
    c. The Groove Line/Heatwave

14. *Our voices will ring together until the twelfth of never.*
    a. How Deep Is Your Love/Bee Gees
    b. We Are the Champions/Queen
    c. Fantasy/Earth, Wind & Fire

15. He *came back to let you know that* he's *got a thing for you* and he *can't let go.*
    a. Bad Case of Loving You/Robert Palmer
    b. What You Won't Do For Love/Bobby Caldwell
    c. Rock With You/Michael Jackson

16. They know *it's a shame,* but they're *giving you back your name.*
    a. You Can't Change That/Raydio
    b. How Much I Feel/Ambrosia
    c. Sail On/Commodores

****

17. They say *you only want to stay with your fancy friends.*
    a. Don't Bring Me Down/Electric Light Orchestra
    b. Livin' It Up (Friday Night)/Bell & James
    c. Heartless/Heart

****

18. *Do you do more than dance?*
    a. Night Moves/Bob Seger & the Silver Bullet Band
    b. Hot Blooded/Foreigner
    c. Dance With Me/Peter Brown

****

19. *There's so oftentimes it happens that we live our lives in chains and we never even know we have the key.*
    a. Dust In the Wind/Kansas
    b. Already Gone/Eagles
    c. Love Will Find a Way/Pablo Cruise

****

20. Their *love is alive, and so it begins.*
    a. Love Takes Time/Orleans
    b. Shake Your Groove Thing/Peaches & Herb
    c. Stumblin' In/Suzi Quatro & Chris Norman

HARDER QUESTIONS: Worth 2 points each — 4 points if you can NAME THAT TUNE without the three choices !

1. *You don't know a good thing when you've got it in your hand.*
   a. Whatcha Gonna Do/Pablo Cruise
   b. Rich Girl/Daryl Hall & John Oates
   c. Slip Slidin' Away/Paul Simon

2. They've *never been with a woman long enough before* their *boots get old.*
   a. Saturday Night Special/Lynyrd Skynyrd
   b. Heard It In a Love Song/Marshall Tucker Band
   c. Deacon Blues/Steely Dan

3. There are times when *questions run too deep for such a simple man.*
   a. The Logical Song/Supertramp
   b. Maybe I'm Amazed/Wings
   c. Love Is the Answer/England Dan & John Ford Coley

4. Because *your sorrow is all* they see, they feel that *if you just want to cry to somebody, don't cry to* them.
   a. Hold the Line/Toto
   b. Hard Luck Woman/Kiss
   c. Strange Way/Firefall

5. *All you got to do is get into the mix if you need a fix.*
   a. Two Out of Three Ain't Bad/Meat Loaf
   b. Rock 'n Roll Never Forgets/Bob Seger
   c. Baby Hold On/Eddie Money

ANSWERS

****

1. a. Used To Be My Girl/O'Jays
2. c. Goodbye Stranger/Supertramp
3. c. When I Need You/Leo Sayer
4. b. Miss You/Rolling Stones
5. b. Copacabana/Barry Manilow
6. c. Knock on Wood/Amii Stewart
7. b. Goodbye Girl/David Gates
8. c. Emotion/Samantha Sang
9. a. Hollywood Nights/Bob Seger & the Silver Bullet Band
10. b. Blame It On The Boogie/Jacksons
11. a. Heaven Knows/Donna Summer
12. b. What's Your Name/Lynyrd Skynyrd
13. a. Take a Chance On Me/Abba
14. c. Fantasy/Earth, Wind & Fire
15. b. What You Won't Do For Love/Bobby Caldwell
16. c. Sail On/Commodores
17. a. Don't Bring Me Down/Electric Light Orchestra
18. b. Hot Blooded/Foreigner
19. b. Already Gone/Eagles
20. c. Stumblin' In/Suzi Quatro & Chris Norman

****

HARDER QUESTIONS--Answers

1. a. Whatcha Gonna Do/Pablo Cruise
2. b. Heard It In a Love Song/Marshall Tucker Band
3. a. The Logical Song/Supertramp
4. c. Strange Way/Firefall
5. b. Rock 'n Roll Never Forgets/Bob Seger

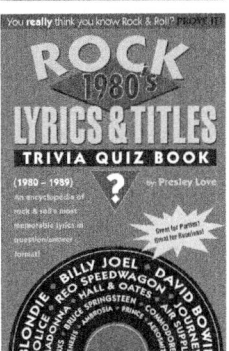

Available on Amazon.com

Printed in Great Britain
by Amazon